Native American & PIONEER SITES of Upstate New York

Native American & PIONEER SITES *of* *Upstate New York*

WESTWARD TRAILS FROM ALBANY TO BUFFALO

LORNA MACDONALD CZARNOTA

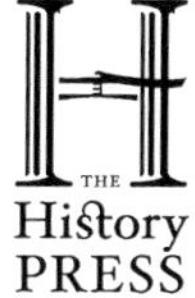

Published by The History Press
Charleston, SC 29403
www.historypress.net

First published 2014

Manufactured in the United States

ISBN 978.1.62619.290.4

Library of Congress CIP data applied for.

Notice: The information in this book is true and complete to the best of our knowledge. It is offered without guarantee on the part of the author or The History Press. The author and The History Press disclaim all liability in connection with the use of this book.

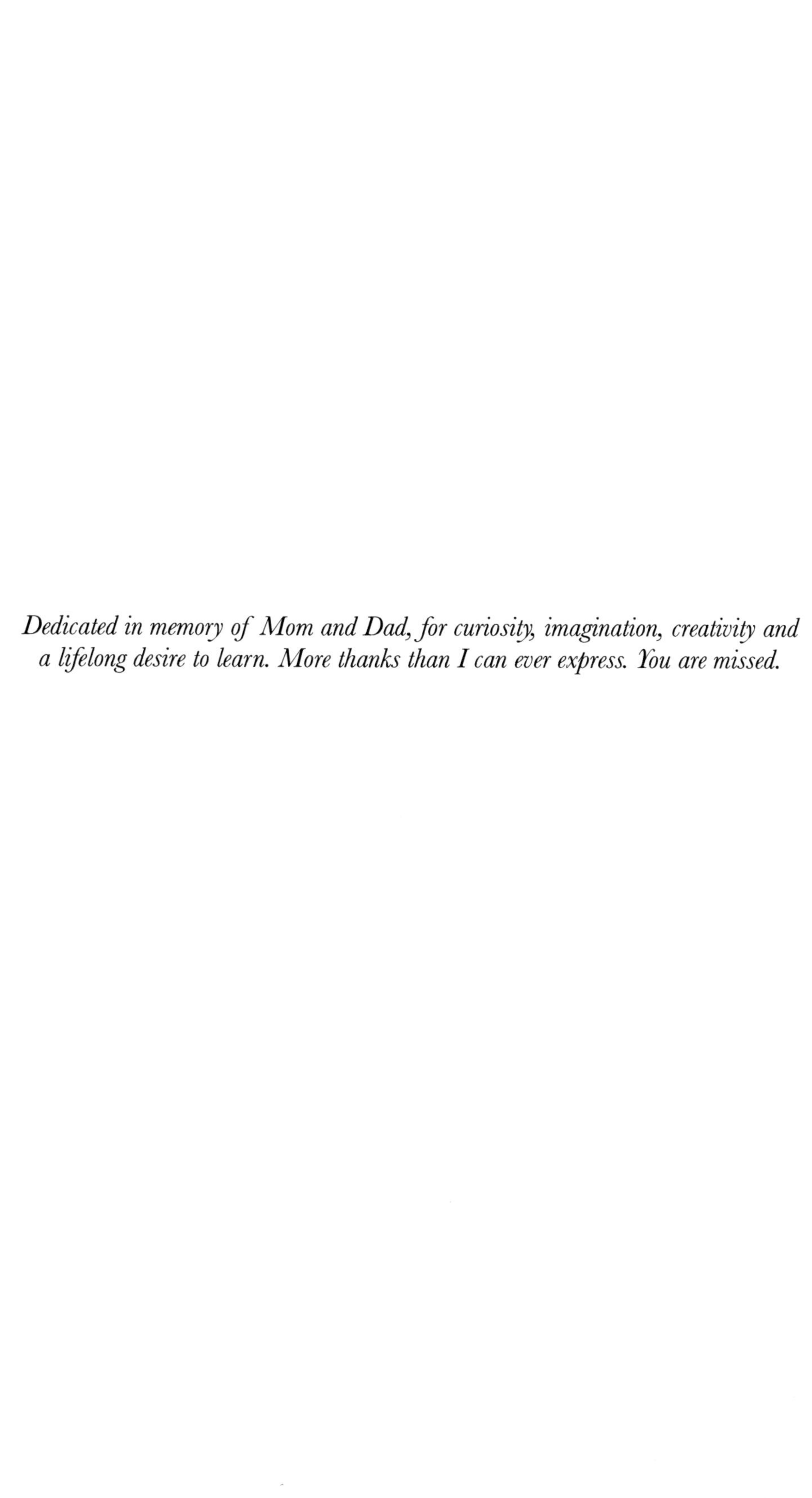

Dedicated in memory of Mom and Dad, for curiosity, imagination, creativity and a lifelong desire to learn. More thanks than I can ever express. You are missed.

CONTENTS

Contents

ACKNOWLEDGEMENTS

I wish to thank the historians and writers who have collected information online and in books about the regions encompassing Routes 5 and 20. Also, thanks to all the entrepreneurs and docents with whom I have spoken over the phone and in person.

Thank you to my editor, Whitney Tarella Landis, Jaime Muehl and the designers from The History Press who always create a beautiful product.

Special thanks to Karen Osburn, archivist for Geneva Historical Society; Glenn Bentz, Iroquois reenactor; James at Avon Historical Society; Pat Reynolds, owner of American Hotel in Lima; and Steve, manager of Holloway House in Bloomfield.

Extra special thanks to the many friends who helped find images for the book, especially Susanna Connelly Holstein, Daniel P. Bronson, Charles Burke and Joan Oblinsky Scharf. Thanks to friend and local artist Alice Gerard for her sketches.

And thank you to my best friend and life partner, Thomas Heim, for the many photographs, keen eye and constant support.

INTRODUCTION

Adventure is worthwhile in itself.
—Amelia Earhart

People who have never been to New York State often think only in terms of New York City, imagining the state to be one large suburb when in fact much of it is very different from the city. The state is mostly rural, bookended by its two largest cities, New York and Buffalo, with Syracuse, Rochester, Binghamton and Albany vying as mid-range urban communities. Many smaller villages lay scattered across the state—or rather, less scattered than purposely placed. The purpose of this book is to explain why these villages exist, how they got their names, what sustained early settlers and what these communities offer us today.

There is no doubt Native American peoples lived in a symbiotic relationship with the environments of New York State. Their many villages are now gone, blended back into the land that they respected. However, their story is not forgotten thanks to the hard work of archaeologists, historians and modern-day Native Americans who work tirelessly to keep that story alive.

We should also remember the early immigrants, who came to find freedoms the Old World did not afford them, and their influences on New York State's landscape. They dared to leave behind the familiar to carve a new nation. While some came because they had no choice and others came for profit, all loved the wilderness beauty they found.

Influenced by water, social change and technological advances, villages grew following the Revolutionary War and during the Industrial Revolution, as well as during the Second Great Awakening. They survived or dwindled yet all have rich legacies in their historical archives. We must know and tell these stories, for they are the foundations of whom we have become.

It is undeniable that building the Erie Canal changed New York State, as did Interstate 90. Today, the Interstate extends over three hundred miles from Buffalo to the Massachusetts border. Using the Thruway makes it easy to bypass the small towns and cities in favor of speed and better gas mileage; however, travelers and history buffs miss a great deal of old-town charm in doing so. Many of the villages located on the two most traveled east–west roads were cutting edge when first settled. Bypassing them changed their faces but not their stories or heritage.

It was not my intention to leave any stories or communities out of this book; however, there are far too many villages and hamlets to mention them all. Hopefully, enough have been included to give a good sense of what it was like living in New York State's wilderness and in villages as they formed, grew or waned. The stories included are a blend of fact and legend, with every effort taken to ensure they are correct.

Most importantly, this book is intended to entice travelers to look deeper at our history and recognize the significant roles these smaller towns played in forging New York State's character. Follow the footsteps of those who came before by way of the westward trails from Albany to Buffalo.

Please visit the author's website for additional photos and stories: www.lornamacdonaldczarnota.com.

ROADS TO A BRAVE NEW WORLD

Once, everything west of Albany was a vast wilderness. With expansion westward shortly after the American Revolution, settlers had two choices of how to cross the state: by waterway or overland. Once simple animal trails and Native American footpaths, Routes 5 and 20 are major thoroughfares today.

Routes 5 and 20, the westward trails, wind between forested hills, previously home to the Iroquois Confederacy. They meander through fertile farmland and utopian playgrounds of the rich. They pass fine vineyards, beautiful Finger Lakes, the Erie Canal, outstanding classical and Victorian architecture and very near to Great Lakes Ontario and Erie. The sites and homes of many Native Americans, early settlers, national heroes, entrepreneurs and inventors overlook these roadways. Who were these people, why did they come here, where have they gone and what legacies have they left us?

Route 5

The stories of Routes 5 and 20 are both shared and unique. These two roads are co-joined for approximately seventy miles from Auburn to Avon. Routes 5 and 20 also travel solo beginning east and west of these two villages. Where Route 20 begins in Massachusetts, Route 5 is born in

Albany. Route 5 and its twin, 5S, lazily parallel the Mohawk River until Route 5 veers off toward Syracuse. Route 20, on the other hand, snakes through the countryside, touching the Finger Lakes on its way to Buffalo and beyond. Route 5 is Main Street throughout much of Western New York, including Batavia, Clarence, Williamsville and Buffalo, to its end near the Pennsylvania border.

Since roads are man-made, they are subject to man's needs and the changes wrought by them. Current-day Route 5 was once called Route 5A. Previously, it was located where current Route 7 can be found. Name changes took place in the 1920s.

Today's Route 5, called the King's Highway during British rule, is an identical parallel to the Great Genesee Road, named as such in 1794, following the Revolution. This road was also known as the Mohawk Trail, Iroquois Trail, Great Indian Trail or Seneca Turnpike. Great Genesee Road predates Route 5 by one hundred years or more. Some of this old road later incorporated Route 5 so that they are indistinguishable. Also following old Indian trails, the Great Genesee Road continued west beyond "settled" lands as far as Fort Niagara. As a formal road, it was meant to serve lands granted to soldiers who participated in the Revolutionary War. It connected Fort Schuyler (Utica, New York) with what is now Caledonia (Canawaugus) in Livingston County. Land companies responsible for handling these grants or tracts demanded better roadways. As a result, four years after being established, the Great Genesee Road was improved and extended to Buffalo. A year prior to its extension, in 1797, a weekly stagecoach began running, eventually leading to many inns and the stagecoach stops servicing them. Of course, when businesses thrive, people begin to build nearby, and towns spring up around them.

While no tolls are charged today, the Great Genesee Road, later the Seneca Turnpike, did once charge tolls to pay for improvements. It was not until completion of the Erie Canal in 1825 that much traffic from the roads reverted to the water. Thus, toll roads became free of charge again.

Route 20

Route 20 is part of the United States transcontinental road system and is the "longest road in the country," running from Boston, Massachusetts, to Newport, Oregon. Over three thousand miles long, it crosses eleven states.

Route 20 is also the longest paved road in New York State. Where Route 5 and 5S pass through or close to large cities, Route 20 bypasses all but Albany. Until the Thruway was built in the 1950s, Route 20 was the main road for east–west travel.

As a major U.S. roadway chartered by the First Great Western Turnpike Corporation when the Revolutionary War ended, Route 20 connected Albany to the village of Cherry Valley. The Cherry Valley section was known as the Cherry Valley Turnpike. Later extensions took the road to Cazenovia and beyond. Many settlers heading west to settle new territories used this route. Stagecoaches began service on Route 20 in 1816.

Because travel on the Erie Canal and railroads was easier, especially for goods, Route 20 was converted from a turnpike, or toll road, back to a free-access road in 1857. The later introduction of Henry Ford's Model T made automobiles affordable to the masses, and as a result of increased travel, New York State took control of paving and maintaining the highways. This would change New York State again, as dirt and rock-strewn roads became pleasant avenues, allowing for leisure as well as business.

Go West Young Man

No horse and cart could have easily navigated the wilderness west of Albany prior to the 1700s. Even walking across New York State, you could not get very far in a day. When Europeans settled the continent, these territories were heavily forested. Footpaths wound through woodlands and along rivers and streams, sometimes marked by natives using a method of bent tree saplings, some of which can still be found throughout New York State's forests, as recorded by naturalist and tree lover Carl Andrew Koehler in his book, *Talking Trees and Spirit Trails*. It is also true that early settlers marked trees so they could navigate their travels, if only to visit a neighbor in this woodland wilderness.

Much early migration was by sleigh across a snow-covered landscape. Though winters could be harsh, roads were more easily traversed with a coating of snow filling in ruts and covering roots. Spring and summer growth made this journey much harder.

Some pioneers did travel by rivers using flat-bottomed boats called bateaux or canoes. Although water made for easier travel in forested lands with few roads, many waterways, including the Mohawk River, held dangerous,

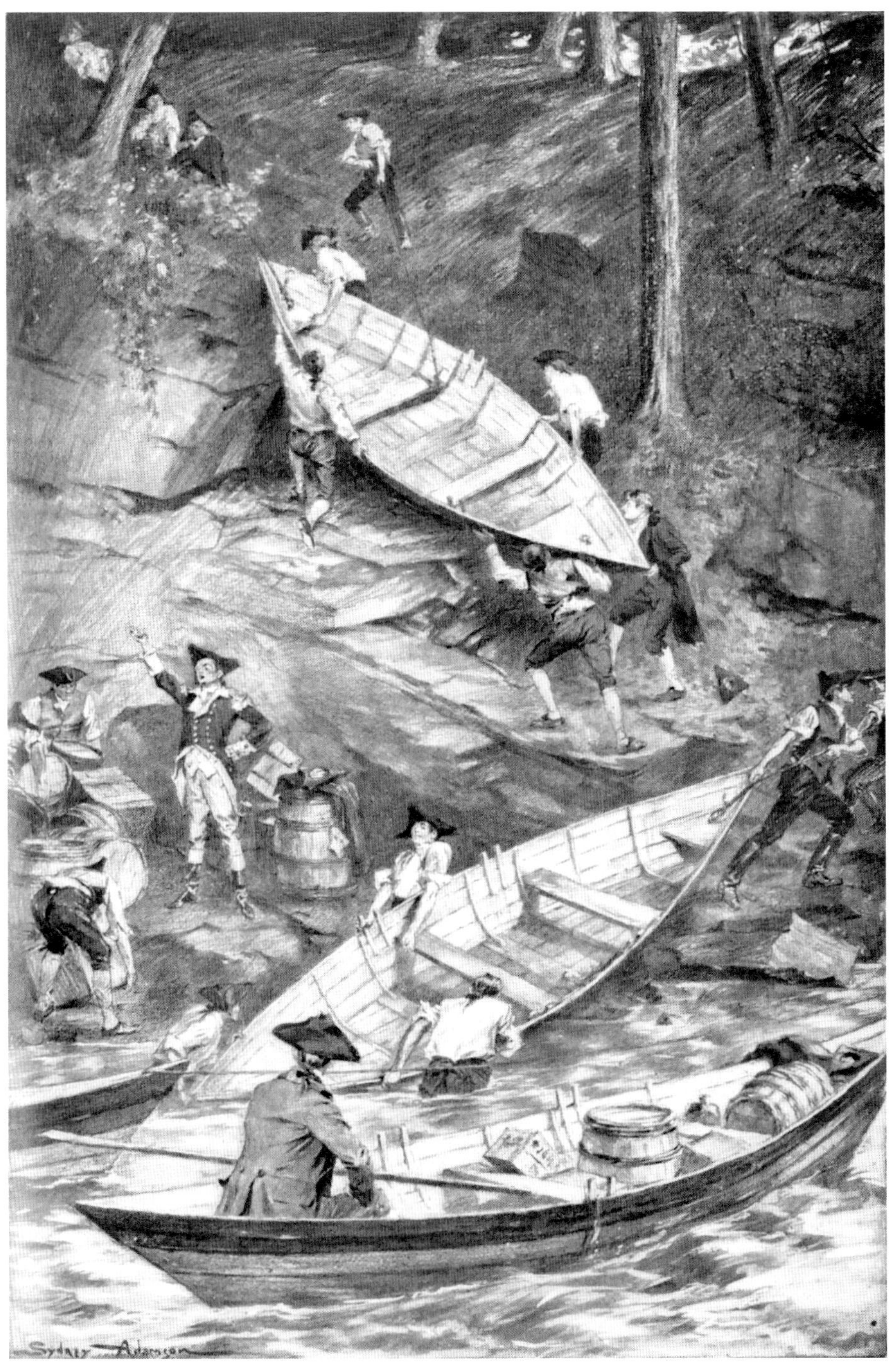

Carrying the bateaux at Skowhegan Falls. *Courtesy of the Library of Congress, Prints and Photographs Division.*

unnavigable expanses. There was just no easy way to transport cargo and passengers into the interior. The Mohawk River, though useful, was not deep enough for heavier boats. Travelers coming to waterfalls or rapids had to portage around them. Many old portage trails used to circumnavigate hazards became our current roads.

The Mohawk River flows eastward, over one hundred miles from its source in the mountains of Lewis County, into the mighty Hudson. It is the Hudson River's largest tributary. Named for a tribe of the Iroquois nation, this river was a key source of fresh water and fish and was used for transportation. Later, European settlers saw its value and built their farms, villages and estates along its shores. However, when Governor Dewitt Clinton broke ground for the Erie Canal in 1817, it was not by way of the Mohawk River as it is today. The land rises almost six hundred feet from the Hudson to Lake Erie. Building a canal was the best way to use water for westward travel, but the technology to build the many locks needed did not exist at affordable costs. Therefore, the early canal paralleled the Mohawk River with aqueducts carrying canal boats over it.

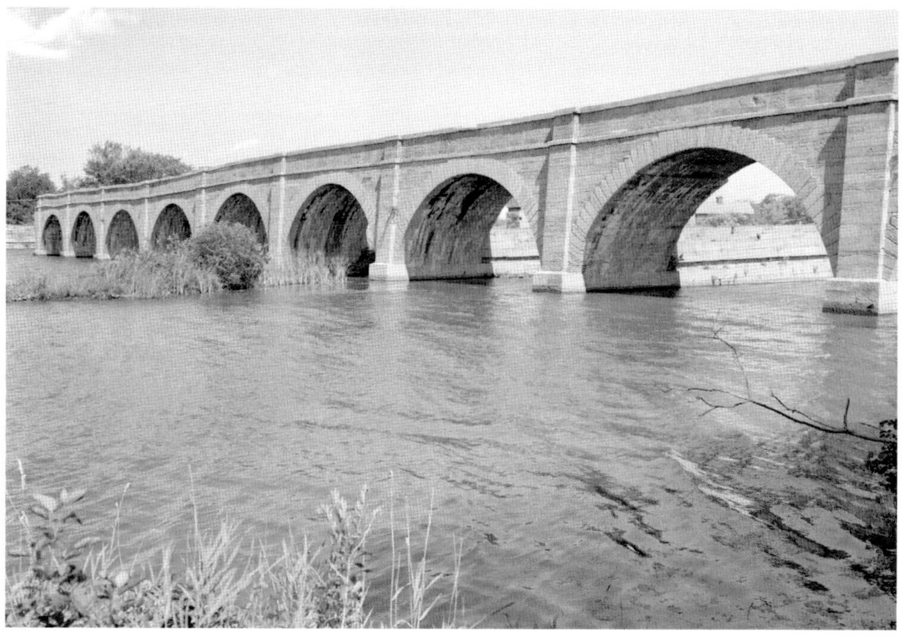

Looking northeast—Erie Canal (enlarged). Schoharie Creek aqueduct, spanning Schoharie Creek, Fort Hunter, Montgomery County, New York. *Courtesy of the Library of Congress, Prints and Photographs Division.*

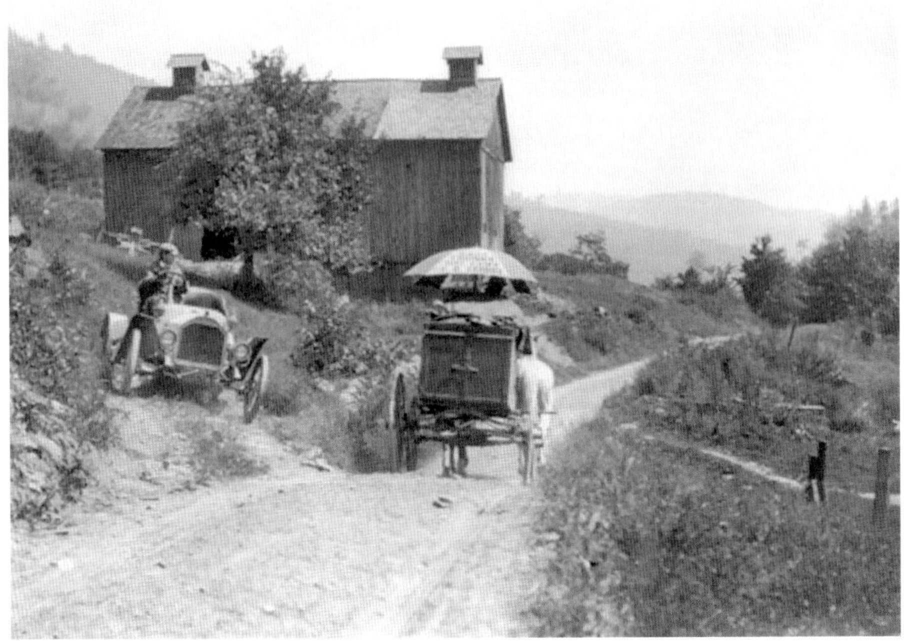

A Buick roadster waits for a horse-drawn wagon to pass on a narrow country road above Liberty, New York. *Courtesy of the Library of Congress, Prints and Photographs Division.*

Once the canal was dug and business flowing, people again gravitated toward the money. Many small towns were settled along the canal. Urban habitation increased rapidly following its completion. Beforehand, more than 85 percent of the state's population was rural.

Beginning about ten years after completion of the Erie Canal, from 1836 to 1862, and again starting in 1903, a series of enlargements took place to transport wider barges and allow for easier two-way traffic. These changes produced the Erie Canal as seen today; some is original, much was moved and a segment is part of the Mohawk River. Once more, the state's face changed. Thriving towns that lost the canal when it was moved dwindled while others along the new canal grew.

As more roads and railroads were completed, travel by water could not compete. People once more turned to overland travel. As more people purchased automobiles, the landscape transformed yet again. This time it was auto camps, motor courts, motels, travel lodges, diners and souvenir gift shops that shaped the experience. Wherever a place of interest could be found, these oases sprouted up. Originally, motorists pulled off roads into town parks to overnight, but without facilities, travelers looked to more convenient establishments. This meant money for towns and entrepreneurs. For earlier pioneers, these conveniences came in the form of taverns and stagecoach stops.

The New Military Tract

Ease of travel and more conveniences motivated later pioneers to make the westward journey, but a truly significant factor leading to the expansion of settlement in New York State came at the end of the Revolutionary War. It was at this time that the federal government made good on its agreement with soldiers who fought until the end of the war. This contract, called the Military Tract, promised land to the soldiers. A new contract by the same name increased the size of these allotments.

The Military Tract was a grant of one hundred acres of land given to each Revolutionary War veteran for his service. Under the "new" grant, these men received an additional five hundred acres—a great deal of land even by today's standards. Since currency was not well trusted, land was a good bargain for soldiers who remained until the war's end.

Twenty-eight townships were established and given a number from one through twenty-eight. These numbers were later swapped for names. Many towns in central New York State have Greek or Roman names, some honoring authors and great intellects. These names might also have paid homage to the governmental systems of Greece and Rome upon which the newly formed nation was based. Naming these townships is attributed to Robert Harpur, a clerk in the state surveyor's office who founded Harpursville, New York. Historians speculate that he had an interest in classical history.

Onondaga and Cayuga Indians also received land in this tract. Sadly, these grants were later reneged upon by the state and contested many times over.

GATEWAYS TO THE WEST

Fort Orange and Schenectady: First Rest Stop

One did not enter the wilderness without first visiting Albany—the farthest western outpost in early New York State. Called Fort Orange at its inception, this colony was named by Henry Hudson for the Netherlands' House of Orange.

In 1664, the Dutch surrendered their territories along the Hudson to England. It was at this time that Fort Orange became Albany and New Amsterdam became New York, both named for English dukes. Britain maintained control of these territories until the Revolution, competing with the French to the west and in Canada for control of the continent and, later, with American Patriots. This longstanding European presence made Albany a large city, central to governance.

Albany, being at the confluence of the Mohawk and Hudson Rivers, became significant for trade, as well as moving pioneers into the country's innermost regions. The first stop in creating this great nation was the Mohawk Valley, which stretches from Albany to current-day Syracuse. Most travelers leaving Albany for the interior would have passed through Schenectady next.

Traveling from Albany to Schenectady was a long day's journey, covering about twenty-eight miles on narrow, rugged footpaths. Schenectady might have been the site of early rest stops for travelers on their way into the wilderness, some of these "permanent" encampments being no more than lean-tos.

Mohawk peoples called the region around Fort Orange *Schaunaughtada*, which the Dutch misinterpreted to mean the "place where the Mohawk River bends." Actually, it meant "on the pine plains." The misinterpretation gave us "Schenectady" at the bend in the river on Route 5. Any nearby native villages were likely early Mohicans, whom Mohawk tribes pushed across the Hudson River prior to the Revolutionary War.

The Dutch first settled Schenectady in 1661. The French and their allied Indian raiders killed these settlers in the winter of 1690. Many succumbed to the cold as they fled to Albany wearing only their nightclothes.

Over a century old by the War for Independence, Schenectady supplied a militia that took part in the Battle of Saratoga and defended Fort Ticonderoga. By then, Queen's Fort, built in 1705, had been torn down and its materials used to build a barracks. A marker in Schenectady shows the previous location of this large fort. The historic neighborhood around it is known as the Stockade District.

Even though the fort was gone, the town was stockaded during the Revolution. It was to Schenectady that many residents of the Mohawk Valley fled when their crops and homes were destroyed during raids.

Like Albany, Schenectady's location made it an ideal port. River bateaux were built here for fur traders and military. Later, in the 1800s, Thomas Edison made it home to his Electric Machine Works. Schenectady eventually became home to General Electric. With its strategic location on the river and the electric business, Schenectady remained a thriving city throughout the Industrial Revolution.

Amsterdam: Shopping Center for Pioneer Settlers

The Dutch settlement of Amsterdam, New York, the next major settlement along Route 5, was largely spared attack by Tories and their allies during the Revolutionary War. This was due to its location at the wilderness edge; Amsterdam was not militarily strategic. Loyalist eyes were set on the valley proper and seats of American government. Amsterdam also lay in proximity to Fort Johnson, a one-time Loyalist stronghold.

Amsterdam's economy fully bloomed only when the Erie Canal was built. Prior to that, industries had primarily served those living nearby.

Streams around Amsterdam powered mills of many kinds. Its proximity to the valley made it a "warehouse" community, selling expendable supplies from the east to settlers in the Mohawk region. Even so, when Scots-Irish and German settlers immigrated prior to the French and Indian War, they disregarded Amsterdam as a place to settle, instead pushing west for land to call their own.

VALLEY OF THE MOHAWK AND THE JESUIT MISSIONARIES

Glacial Lake Iroquois

The peaceful, fertile Mohawk Valley began with the turbulent end of the last ice age. Lake Ontario, Lake Oneida and the Mohawk River are all that remain of a once more expansive lake known to geologists as Glacial Lake Iroquois. This enormous body of water, part of a vast ocean, was one of many created by melting glaciers. It fed from early Lake Erie.

In a simplified perspective, Glacial Lake Iroquois was approximately one hundred feet above current-day Lake Ontario. As ice melted, the glacial lake drained down mountains near Rome, New York. Its natural path would have been via the St. Lawrence River, but an ice jam blocked the river. Rushing with great force, these lake waters carried sediment, carving out potholes, plains and plateaus, toward Glacial Lake Albany. This created the corridor that became the Mohawk River Valley before flowing on to the Hudson River. It was a dance of water and rock that lasted thousands of years, resulting in the beautiful landscape the Mohawk Indians called home.

The Mohawks: "The People of Flint"

The story of the Mohawk people is synonymous with the Mohawk Valley and its eventual settlement by the Europeans. It was in the valley that white immigrants to the state first encountered the Iroquois and from here that the native population of the country would begin its transformation.

The Iroquois viewed their lands as a great longhouse. There was an eastern door where the sun rose and a western door where it set. The Senecas kept the Western Door. The Mohawks were the "Keepers of the Eastern Door." This symbolism dates back over five hundred years. The longhouse represented community, and everyone in a longhouse had a role—they worked together. This common metaphor united the Six Confederacy tribes. They understood and revered it. Yet the longhouse would also contribute to the Mohawks' destruction.

Two great men are attributed as founders of the Iroquois Confederacy—Dekanawida, the "Great Peacemaker," and legendary chief Hiawatha. Little is known of their personal lives. Most of their story has passed down to us as legend, with conflicting reports of their births and whether they were of the Mohawk nation or adopted into it. However, few dispute the success of their concept to join five nations into one cohesive organization. These five were the Mohawk, Oneida, Onondaga, Cayuga and Seneca tribes, all people who warred with one another for centuries. They became brothers under the Confederacy. The Tuscarora joined more than a century later. This union made the Mohawks stronger, saving them from total desolation. Only the Revolutionary War would break this brotherhood.

Throughout the 1600s, the Mohawks are reported to have governed over eleven million acres or approximately seventeen thousand square miles from south of the St. Lawrence River to the Delaware, from Lake Champlain to West Canada and south to Unadilla Creek. These lands were claimed by centuries of occupation. The Mohawk Valley was their capital region. Their greatest threats, until white settlers arrived, were the Algonquins and other northern tribes that constantly attempted to push into Mohawk hunting grounds.

Prior to 1650, the Mohawk nation's population might have been as many as eight thousand people, not including the rest of the Confederacy that would have allied itself to the Mohawks in times of war. Theirs was a strong, mostly self-sufficient society.

The Mohawks created the valley's first economy and were the first builders of great villages. These villages, called "castles" by the Dutch, straddled the Mohawk River, becoming centers for commerce, social activity and council fires. According to Jesuit records, there were three primary Mohawk castles: Ossernonon (Turtle clan), Andagaron (Bear clan) and Tionontoguen (Wolf clan). These three were originally located on the river's south side along

Route 5S but later moved north of the river. All told, there might have been as many as seven large villages.

Routes following the waterways and mountain ridges were important. Rivaled for transit by only the St. Lawrence River, the Mohawk River was the Iroquois' most significant trail to interior regions. Yet even this major waterway would be part of the Mohawk nation's demise, as it carried white men and their diseases.

Illness traveled quickly in longhouses holding upward of one hundred people, especially when several of these were placed in proximity to one another in more populated villages. Add to this the Mohawk River's easy access and an influx of Christian missionaries into the valley and you have a deadly combination.

A smallpox epidemic spread throughout the valley between the years 1661 and 1663. By the end of this period, the Mohawk population was decimated to fewer than two thousand people, making it vulnerable not only to other tribes but also to Europeans, who would force the natives to choose sides in their conflicts.

In order to stem the steady decrease in population, the Mohawks integrated new policies. They repopulated with adopted captives, watering down bloodlines but not ending their existence. In addition, to maintain a peaceful existence, the Mohawks signed treaties with the French and, later, with others. While this did bring them peace, it also proved fatal to their standing as the most powerful landholders in New York State. Little by little, they were stripped of their property. So went their wealth and voice, until at last, the Mohawk would be forced into Canada.

The Beaver Wars occurred during the mid-1600s among neighbouring Indian nations for control over lucrative trade in beaver pelts. This spilled over into a conflict that also involved the French, who largely controlled Canada and had established themselves in the fur trade as middlemen between the Indians and European merchants. The Mohawks of New York State sold their furs to the Dutch, who settled the Hudson River regions, and to the British, while the French traded with the Mohawks' rivals, the Hurons. This further established the French as enemies to the Mohawks, who saw the Hurons becoming stronger by way of this relationship with the French. The Mohawks felt they had no recourse but to attack the French just as they did any others who encroached on their way of life or threatened their existence. With their powerful position in the Iroquois Confederacy, the Mohawks seemed unstoppable as they gained land during this time. However, North America's entire native population would be affected by this struggle.

Raiding parties of Iroquois attacked isolated farms and settlements in French territories, taking captives to be adopted. Even with almost equal numbers of Hurons and Algonquins allied to the French, the Mohawks appeared stronger. However, following a series of attacks in the 1650s, including those in which the Mohawks took part in blockades of Montreal and Quebec, the French brutally pushed back. It took ten years, but the French finally struck deep into Mohawk territory. In January 1666, a French invasion force of four to five hundred men marched south into the valley heartland. This initial invasion was halted, but the French took a valuable hostage: Chief Canaqueese of Mohawk-Dutch ancestry.

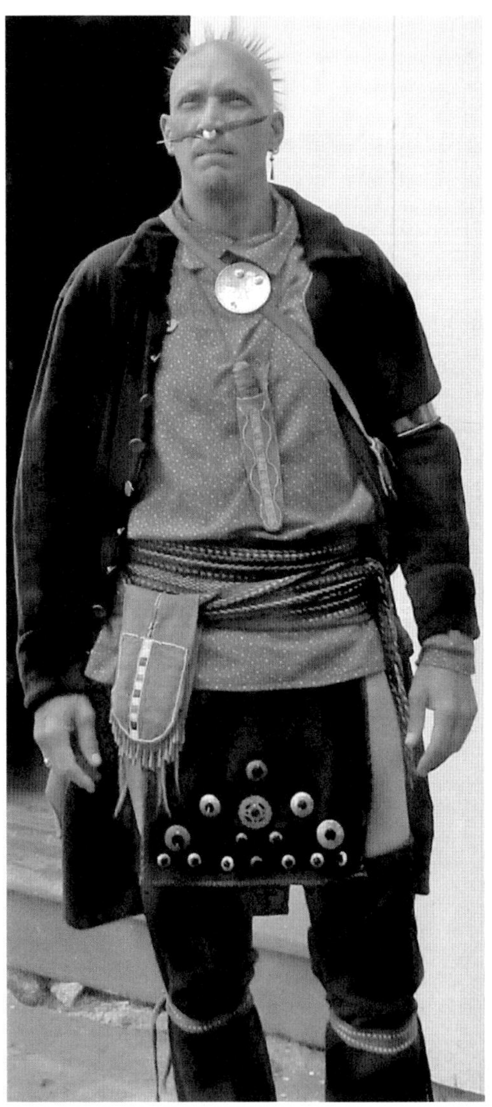
Iroquois reenactor. *Courtesy of the author, with permission.*

Emboldened, in the autumn of 1666, a force more than twice as large as the last entered Mohawk lands. Knowing of this invasion, the Mohawks moved their women and children from their villages. The French burned all homes and crops in these deserted communities. Nothing was spared. Prouville de Tracy seized all Mohawk lands in the name of France and forced the Mohawks to sign a treaty. (Twenty years later, Denonville would repeat these actions against the Senecas in the state's western regions.)

With their homes and food supply destroyed and winter coming, the Mohawks had little choice. Yet this treaty was more than a peace treaty with the French and their allied Indians; it was also a promise to allow Jesuit missionaries into their villages. Thus, Christianity entered the Mohawk Valley. Chief Canaqueese was freed to gather his scattered people with a dire warning from de Tracy: should the Mohawks attempt future raids, de Tracy would not hold back his wrath.

Many Mohawk people died from cold and starvation that winter.

As a result of the white man's politics and policies, and the effects of illness and harsh conditions, the once great villages of the Iroquois people can be seen only in our imaginations. If history had taken a different turn, perhaps we could still visit and trade with the Mohawk castles of the valley.

Burnt-Face Girl: A Legend

An Algonquin legend, specifically Micmac, tells of a miraculous event, one that is similar in nature to a miracle performed by the Mohawk Valley's Kateri Tekakwitha, first Native American saint.*

There was once a great Indian village built near a great forest lake. At the far end of this village, separate from all the rest, was the longhouse of a mighty hunter. He was called Invisible One because only his sister, who cooked and tended his lodge, could see him. Invisible One was strong and handsome. His hunting skills made him a good potential husband, but only a girl who could see him could marry him. Many village girls wanted Invisible One for their husband. Many tried, all failed.

Now in this same village, there lived an old man and his three daughters. The youngest was her father's favorite, but compared to the other two, she was meek and small—an easy target for their teasing and their tricks. As the three grew, the youngest remained loveliest and kindest, too, even though constantly tormented by her older sisters. That torment turned to outright torture.

One day, the older sisters held their younger sibling, cutting her long, lush hair so that it was short and ragged. When their old father returned

---

*. The Burnt-Face Girl is one of many Cinderella variants known as Invisible One and Strong Wind. There are several versions of this story, and one can be found at the following: "The Algonquin Legends of New England, or, Myths and Folk Lore of the Micmac, Passamaquoddy, and Penobscot Tribes" by Charles Godfrey Leland, https://archive.org/details/cihm_04575.

to the lodge, she fell crying in his arms. He asked who had done such a terrible thing. Her sisters replied, "She was mad and cut it herself." The same happened when the girls used hot coals to burn their sister's arms and legs and even scar her lovely face.

"She is mad!" they told their father. "She has done this to herself."

They hid all the beautiful clothes their father gave his youngest daughter when he traded. "These, too," they said, "she has thrown away."

The poor girl got no rest when her father was gone nor justice or sympathy when her sisters lied. The people called her *Oochigeaska*, "Rough-Face" or "Burnt-Face." Yet all three girls grew to be young women, with Oochigeaska kinder of heart each day.

Then came a time when the older sisters desired to try to win Invisible One for their own. First, the eldest walked along the lakeshore past the hunter's longhouse. As was her custom, Invisible One's sister was waiting and walked by her side. When she saw her brother coming home, she asked the village girl, "Of what is his shoulder strap made?"

The oldest sister replied, "Of rawhide."

Of course, she was wrong. This girl, like all the rest who came before her, could not see the warrior and was sent home in shame. The middle sister also tried but was turned away. It seemed Invisible One would always be a bachelor.

Oh, whatever was Oochigeaska thinking in that foolish little scarred head of hers when she decided that she, of all people, should seek the hunter's lodge!

Burnt-face girl had no moccasins. Her sisters had taken them. She wore an old pair of her father's that flipped and flopped and flapped as she walked. And no clothes! What could she wear except bark given to her by the birch trees in the nearby forest? These she cleverly sewed into a ridiculous dress and leggings that rustled as she swayed. Her hair was a ragged misshapen mass on top of her head! Everyone hissed and laughed as she walked through the village. Her sisters were horrified. She would shame them all. Yet off the brave girl went with her head held high, down to the lakeshore, down past Invisible One's longhouse.

As always, the warrior's sister met the girl who walked there. She did not laugh or ridicule her. She only waited until her brother returned home then asked her question, "Do you see my brother?"

"I do," Burnt-Face answered, "and he is wonderful."

"Of what is my brother's shoulder strap made?"

"Oh," exclaimed Burnt-Face. "It is made of the rainbow."

"And, my sister, what is his bowstring?"

"The Spirit's Road, the Milky Way."

Oochigeaska could see him!

Invisible One's sister took Burnt-Face by the hand. She led her into the water, where she was bathed. When the water touched her skin, the scars were washed away. The sister combed Oochigeaska's hair, and it grew back long and shiny. She was given a beautiful dress and leggings of fine white deerskin and then taken to meet the man she would marry. Oh, it was a joyous occasion for all three—Oochigeaska, Invisible One and his sister. Of course, they lived happily ever after.

Some versions of this story call the handsome hunter Strong Wind, saying that when he asked his new wife who had tortured her and discovered it was her sisters, he turned them into aspen trees who shake when Strong Wind passes by.

This story does not belong to the Mohawk people, but it is curiously similar to the story of one of the valley's most famed native women, the Blessed Kateri, whose story is connected with the villages of Fonda and Auriesville.

Before arriving at these villages, travelers might pass through the tiny hamlet of Tribes Hill, a later native site.

Ogsadaga: Tribes Hill

Traveling westward from Amsterdam, New York, past Fort Johnson, one will find the community of Tribes Hill. This is where the Mohawks built their collective village of Ogsadaga after French and Indian forces burned them out in 1693. Seven years later, the Mohawks established three major castles (stockaded villages) at the sites of today's Fort Hunter, Fort Plain and Indian Castle. They left these castles in 1775 at the start of the Revolution. The community of Tribes Hill retained its connection to this early native village through its name. Its name makes it rare among the other villages of the valley, which were named mostly for founders.

Fonda, New York: The Shrine of Kateri Tekakwitha and Caughnawaga

Approximately five miles west of Tribes Hill is a small village named for its founder, Douw Fonda, who settled there in 1750 and operated a trading post. Deeply rooted in agriculture and the dairy industry, the village became a center for cheese making. There were also many mills, including a woollen mill that was taken over in the early 1900s by Congressman Lucius Littauer of Gloversville (a center for glove making). The factory then became Fonda Glove Lining Company. The village of Fonda, like many others, grew with the Erie Canal and waned with its passing.

Many people might not realize that Hollywood star Henry Fonda, who played the lead role in *Drums Along the Mohawk* as well as in many other box office successes, traced his ancestry to Douw Fonda. When Henry Fonda died, Fonda, New York, lowered its flags to half-staff as a show of affection. The village is best known today as the location of the shrine to the Blessed Kateri Tekakwitha, first Native American saint. She lived at nearby Caughnawaga with her family after Ossernonon, the village of her birth, was destroyed by Prouville de Tracy.

Caughnawaga was a significant Mohawk village, the name meaning "at the wild waters." Built to replace Ossernonon, this new village was located on a plateau overlooking the valley and remained inhabited until 1693. Archaeologists rediscovered Caughnawaga in 1950, and it is now an

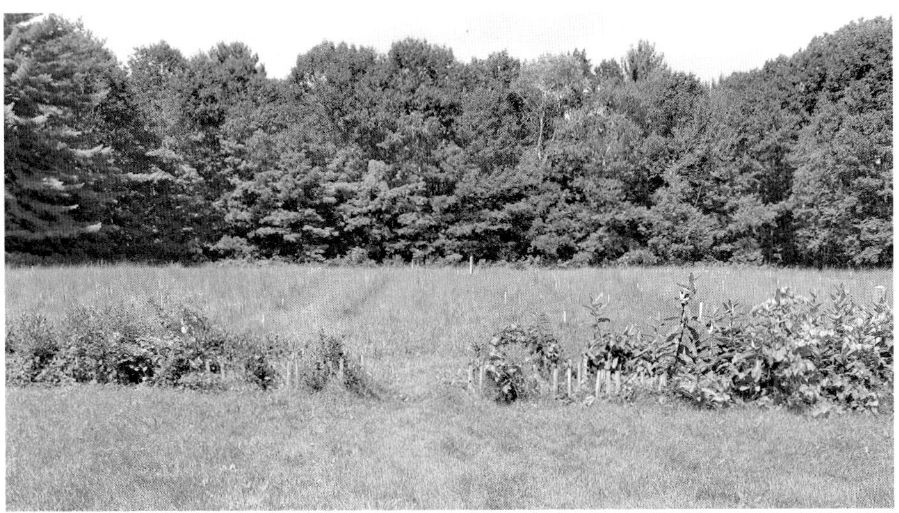

Archeological site of the native village of Caughnawaga. *Courtesy of the author.*

archaeological site. Many postholes for the stockade have been marked, as have locations of its longhouses, but little else remains.

Following his punitive actions against the Mohawks, Prouville de Tracy forced them to sign a treaty that allowed missionaries within the native villages. Once the village was completed, Caughnawaga became a permanent Jesuit mission, but this did not save it from attack by rival natives, particularly the Mahicans (Mohicans). An Algonquin tribe, the Mahicans were settled around Albany, just east of the valley. On a morning in August 1669, in the pre-dawn hours, they staged a siege against Caughnawaga Castle that lasted three days.

Mohawk warriors were roused from sleep and manned the protective palisade as quickly as they could move. The enemy had already opened fire. Mohawk scouts were sent to warn castles to the west. It was noon before reinforcements reached Caughnawaga. In a valiant effort with the newly arrived support, the Mohawk warriors burst out through the gate. The Mohicans retreated into the nearby forest after retrieving their dead. Many Mohawks were killed or injured in this first assault. Father Pierron, a Jesuit priest stationed at Caughnawaga, tended the wounded with help from some of the women, including twelve-year-old Kateri Tekakwitha. Two more days of attack followed.

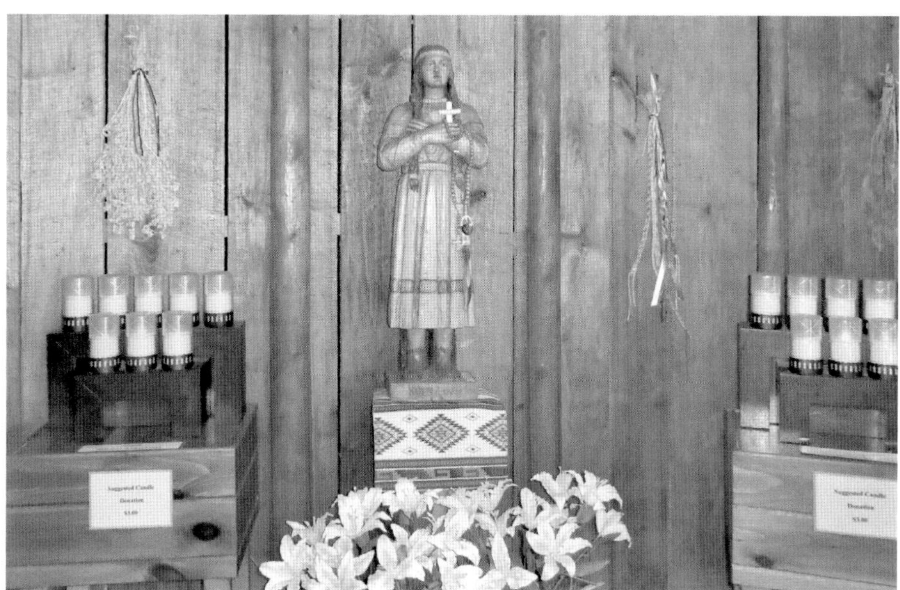

Shrine of Saint Kateri Tekakwitha, interior altar. *Courtesy of the author.*

Caughnawaga's Mohawks were well supplied, but not so the Mohicans. Their supplies, including ammunition, began to run low. By this time in history, traditional native bows had been replaced with European guns, and bullets were not as easy to come by as arrows. This forced the Mohicans to retreat once again from the village, though they didn't go far. They took up position on a summit where they could watch the path below for the Mohawk war party following them. The Mohawks had been depleted in number even before this attack, so they waited for additional reinforcements from other castles before setting out in pursuit.

The Mohawks easily caught up with their enemy, who were waiting in ambush. They fought for two days before a runner arrived at Caughnawaga with word that they had succeeded in driving the Mohicans back. Father Pierron set off immediately to help the wounded at the site of this battle.

Many Mohicans were taken captive. According to writings from Father Pierron, these captives were tormented at the battle site and then taken to Caughnawaga, where they were forced to walk the gauntlet, tortured further and killed or burned alive. Father Pierron could not allow this to take place without giving them last rites. He prepared them for death with baptism.

Once the siege ended and healing began, Father Pierron convinced many of the Indians to convert to Christianity. Many of the earliest converts were women, Kateri Tekakwitha among them.

Auriesville: Ossernonon and the North American Martyrs

Auriesville is a hamlet located about forty miles west of Albany on the Mohawk River's southern shore and Route 5S. Supposedly named for the last Mohawk man who lived there, it is the location of the Shrine of the North American Martyrs, founded by a priest of St. Joseph's parish in Troy, New York, sometime before 1884. The shrine was originally superimposed over ten acres of the destroyed native village of Ossernonon, birthplace of Saint Kateri Tekakwitha, who was born there in 1656. The holy site has since undergone changes and expansion.

The first shrine built on the site was called Our Lady of Martyrs. The grounds were extended to four hundred acres in 1930. Today's coliseum shrine can hold up to six thousand people. Over four thousand pilgrims travel there each summer.

One might also find a Jesuit cemetery nearby, and the surroundings are undeniably imbued with the spirit of its early history, tragic though it may be. Ossernonon is gone, but one can sense it sleeping just beneath the surface.

Indian raiding parties were commonplace. This was also true of the Mohawk Indians who raided neighboring tribes as far away as Canada. Some of these raids were revenge attacks; some were over resources, including the human kind. It can be difficult to discern why some captives were killed while others were enslaved or adopted. Captives often took the places of family members killed in battle or by illness. In the case of the three North American Martyrs, death was most likely because they refused to submit to the native way. Reports of Isaac Jogues, Jean de Lalande and René Goupil suggest that they were peaceful men, gentle teachers and healers, though we cannot know the opinion of the natives at that time beyond the writings of white witnesses.[*]

René Goupil became a Jesuit lay brother as a young man. When he arrived from France at New France in Canada, he submitted himself fully to the will of his superior, who taught the lay brother through hard work and self-sacrifice. Goupil proved himself worthy after spending two years serving the household at menial tasks. He was then tasked with caring for patients in the hospital, becoming a skilled surgeon.

The winter of 1641 was harsh, with many crops failing, so Isaac Jogues, a veteran priest serving in Huronia (southern Ontario today), led an expedition to Trois-Rivières (Three-Rivers, Canada) and Quebec to obtain supplies. When it was time to leave, Jogues requested that Goupil join him. He felt that Goupil's skills would be useful among the Hurons who traveled with them and to those in villages where they planned to trade. In a letter sent to Father Jérôme Lalemant in early May 1646, Jogues described Goupil as joyful for having been called upon. Jogues knew well what dangers awaited them. René Goupil did not.

After a successful mission, they left Trois-Rivières on August 1 to return to Huronia. Jogue, Goupil, possibly three other Frenchmen and their small

*. The "Jesuit Relations" are made up of many volumes of reports made by the Jesuits regarding their activities in the New World. The information used for this book was found online at the following: "The Jesuit Relations and Allied Documents, Travels and Explorations of the Jesuit Missionaries in New France 1610–1791," http://puffin.creighton.edu/jesuit/relations/relations_31.html.

band of Hurons had only just begun their homeward journey when they met a Mohawk raiding party. The Hurons fled, leaving the peaceful Jesuits to be captured. Jogues writes that while they waited as some of their captors pursued the fleeing Hurons, Goupil submitted his will to God. Jogues, less naïve than his companion, heard his confession.

Reports of the Jesuits' torture are gruesome; most of the Huron prisoners were killed after receiving baptism from Father Jogues. Although he urged Goupil to flee, Goupil would not leave Jogues' side, just as Jogues would not leave those in his charge. Father Jogues later wrote of his fellow Jesuit's courage and piety. The two priests were tormented for six days as they marched toward Ossernonon, their final destination.

Finally, after being held for six weeks, Jogues and Goupil were called into the village proper to attend their verdict. Brother Goupil held on to hope that they might be released to Trois-Rivières, but Jogues knew better. He urged Goupil to make himself ready, and they said their final prayers. They had only just set foot at the village gate when a tomahawk struck Goupil's head. Two more blows killed him on that September 28. Jogues was taken to a lodge established as his during their captivity.

Father Jogues sought to bury his fallen comrade. With help from a native captive, Jogues risked everything to go outside village walls to search for Goupil. They found him stripped of his clothes and dragged by the neck to a nearby stream. His body had been partially eaten by animals. They weighted the remains down under the water to keep it safe from further desecration. However, it was found by his captors and taken into the woods, where it fed the flora and fauna. It would be another season, into spring, before Jogues could search for the body again. He hid what bones he found.

A letter to Father Lalemant explained that Goupil was killed because he had made the sign of the cross on a native child. Jogues cited him as a martyr. This same letter is part of an expansive collection of reports known as the "Jesuit Relation," the only early written accountings of these events.

The intention for the remaining prisoners was to burn them alive. Somehow, perhaps by way of a fleeing Huron, word of the events reached the Dutch settlement of New Amsterdam. A ransom was arranged, but the Mohawks rejected it. However, this offer might have been what saved Jogues and the rest. Instead of killing them, the Mohawks decided to wait for a better offer.

Jogues was a slave at Ossernonon for more than a year. In that time, he occasionally wandered into the nearby woods to pray, even in the harsh winter months. He gained respect among his captors. There was one old woman he called "aunt." She helped him stay alive by healing his wounds and warning him of danger. It is said Jogues baptized seventy people during that year.

The only sin I can remember during my captivity is that I sometimes looked on the approach of death with complacency.

—Father Isaac Jogues

What took the Dutch so long to set him free? They cultivated a peaceful relationship with the Mohawks for fur trade and did not wish to risk jeopardizing their agreements. Finally, a solution presented itself. The Dutch invited the Mohawks to bring the Jesuit priest to Fort Orange (Albany). Secretly, Father Jogues was informed upon his arrival at the fort that a ship was being made ready to carry him to France. Early in the dawning hours of the following day, the Jesuit quietly slipped away from his Indian guards, rowed to the waiting ship and sailed away to safety. The Mohawks

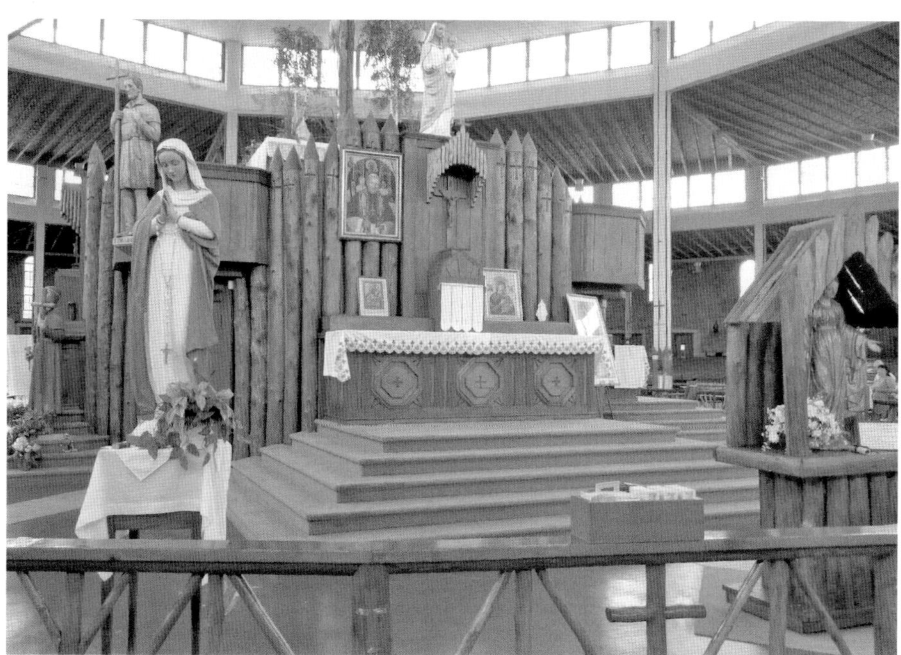

Shrine of the North American Martyrs, interior altar. *Courtesy of the author.*

threatened the Dutch for helping Jogues escape, though nothing came of the threat. Jogues eventually reached his homeland. His tale might have ended here, except that Father Jogues was once more sent to Canada in 1644, this time to Montreal.

In 1646, a contingent of Iroquois had traveled to Canada with the promise of a truce and a desire to ransom prisoners. Father Lalemant decided Jogues should go again into the Mohawk interior on this peace mission. We can only imagine the immense courage Jogues must have summoned after all he had endured at Mohawk hands, though it is said he was glad to go, harboring no ill will. Father Lalemant felt at ease knowing Jogues knew the dangers and the Mohawk way.

The first leg of his six-week mission was traveled with Father Bourdon. They delivered their entreaties and then returned to Montreal in May. However, Jogues felt uneasy in Montreal, as if he had more to do. In late September, he decided to return to Mohawk territory. This time, Father Jogues did not return home. This time, he became a martyr, as did his companion, Jean de Lalande.

Jean de Lalande, a lay brother like Goupil, was to accompany Jogues. He might have been attached to the settlement of Trois-Rivières, which was very near the eventual Indian Christian village of Kahnawake. Unlike Goupil, Lalande was more emotionally sedate. Some stories say he had little knowledge of the dangers of this mission. Surely, he must have heard tales of Goupil and Jogues. Nevertheless, he did his duty toward his superiors.

The journey began in the last days of September. Father Jogues, Brother Lalande and a few Hurons traveled from Trois-Rivières southward. As they moved deeper into Mohawk lands, they began to hear rumors that some of the Mohawk nation planned to break the brittle truce at their first opportunity. The party was advised to turn back. As on his first expedition in 1642, all but one of Jogues' Hurons abandoned him. The two priests continued alone, even though Jogues had premonitions of his death:

> *My heart tells me that if I am the one to be sent on this mission I shall go but I shall not return. But I would be glad if our Lord wished to complete the sacrifice where He began it. Farewell, dear Father. Pray that God unite me to Himself inseparably.*

News of Jogues' death on October 18, 1646, reached Quebec the following summer. A letter from Governor Kieft at Fort Orange told how the Jesuits were beaten and tomahawked—first Jogues and then Lalande the following day as he attempted to retrieve Jogues' body. Many misfortunes and illness had befallen the Mohawks, and according to Father Lalemant in the "Jesuit Relation" for 1647, the natives blamed the Christians for these ailments. No details are given of the priests' suffering. Unlike Goupil, for whom Jogues had stood witness, nobody with written language was there to chronicle Jogues' story.

In 1930, Pope Pius XI declared Jogues, Lalande and Goupil to be saints. Five other Canadians were named as well, but only these three and Kateri Tekakwitha are honored at the North American Shrine in Auriesville, New York, once called Ossernonon (Lower Mohawk Castle).

Twenty-plus years passed following the deaths of the Jesuit missionaries at Ossernonon, and life for the Mohawks of the valley was mostly peaceful among the forests and small mountains, with the constant presence of the nearby river. Yet tragedy would strike at the very heart of the Mohawk people, and it came by way of the Europeans.

Throughout Kateri Tekakwitha's young life, many native refugees of wars and retaliatory attacks migrated into the valley. Then, in 1660, smallpox ravaged the villages, including Ossernonon. This is where Kateri's story of ordeal begins, as her family died, and she was terribly scarred and blinded, yet her troubles were not hers alone. The smallpox epidemic killed many children, decreasing the Mohawk people's future population. However, smallpox was not the only event that changed the native way of life; in fact, another would have an even more profound effect: the arrival of Prouville de Tracy.

When Prouville de Tracy entered the valley in 1666 to punish the Mohawks for their attacks on French settlements, he burned Ossernonon along with its crops. Already weakened by smallpox, the village was no match for de Tracy's forces. Many natives hid in a nearby forest until the troops were gone. Families took what shelter they could throughout that winter, which is said to have been particularly harsh. These now homeless natives crossed to the Mohawk River's north shore and began building their new village of Caughnawaga.

Thus was the end of Ossernonon as a trading center for the Mohawk. Today, we can walk the grounds of the Shrine to the North American Martyrs, view and observe the stations of the cross and other monuments and enter the Coliseum, but beyond imagination, the native presence is lost.

A NEW FACE IN THE VALLEY

A trickling immigration of white settlers followed Christianization of the Mohawk Indians, as well as two major wars for control of lands that first belonged to these natives, changing their lives forever. It was no longer a matter of thriving from the land and protecting it from neighboring tribes. Now it became a matter of choosing sides among the white men in order to keep the tribe from complete extinction. Although forced from the region by their choices, the Mohawks' ruin might have happened sooner if not for the committed fellowship between the natives and Indian agent Sir William Johnson.

Sir William Johnson: Brother to the Indian, Businessman, Frontier Developer, Military Leader

Prior to the Revolutionary War, William Johnson was the Mohawk Valley's favorite son. He was the French and Indian War hero who named Lake George and captured Fort Niagara, and he was the valley's wealthiest landowner. It was because of his efforts that the Mohawks sided with the British in both conflicts.

Although a Loyalist, Johnson dealt honestly with his native brothers, sometimes to the brink of subordination with his superiors. Even so, British

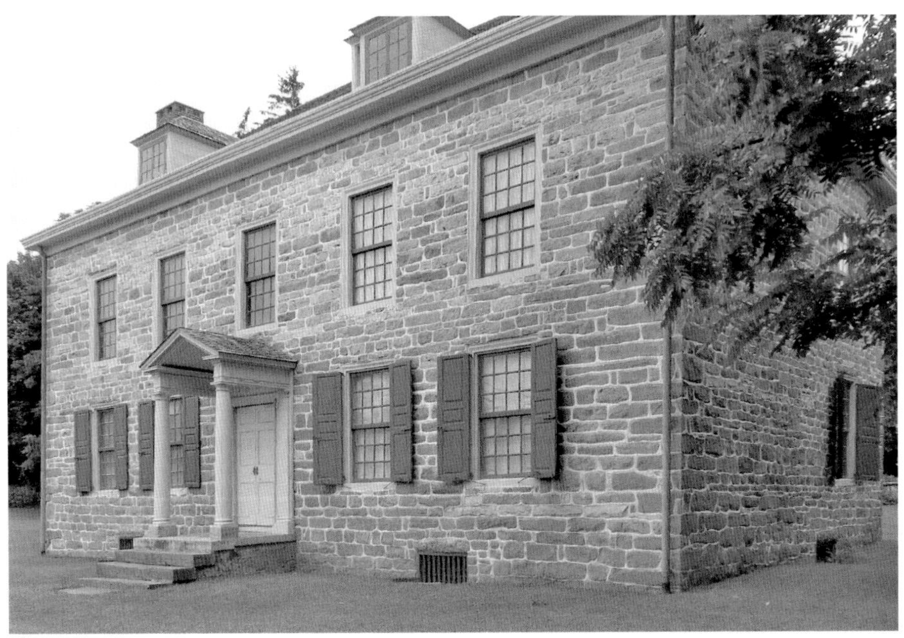

Fort Johnson, first valley home of Sir William Johnson. *Courtesy of the author.*

military leadership saw Johnson's position with the Indians as one that could only further its desires toward complete dominion on the continent. His influence among the Indians continued even after his death, thanks to his powerful native common-law wife, Molly (Mary) Brant.

William Johnson was a young man when he left his homeland of Ireland for the colonies. His uncle Peter Warren, an established landowner in the Mohawk Valley, employed William to develop that land. William brought several families to lease parcels of his uncle's property. As per his uncle's wishes, William set up trade with the Indians, but not near Warrensburgh, where his uncle had planned. (This Warrensburgh is not the same as current-day Warrensburgh, located in the Adirondacks. The name was most likely changed or the site disbanded following the war. It was on the river's southern side, possibly within sight of Fort Johnson on the opposite shore.)

Always with a keen eye for opportunity, William noticed heavier traffic on the Mohawk River's northern trail. It made more sense to him to build a trading post along that path. In 1739, Johnson bought a house and established his trading post and a sawmill. His business at "Mount Johnson" (later called Fort Johnson) flourished, especially when his dealings eliminated middlemen between the Indians and Albany merchants. Johnson dealt directly with

Albany businesses. Though he alienated himself from his uncle and others in this way, his connection with the Indians deepened. Johnson's fairness with them won a trust between them that established William Johnson in a league of his own, the likes of which the Iroquois had not experienced with white men before.

As a result of good business dealings, Governor Clinton of New York gave William Johnson the task of supplying Fort Oswego. William became superintendent of Indian affairs in 1755. The Indians truly considered William Johnson a friend in their negotiations with the white man. Perhaps the high watermark for Johnson came when the natives under his commission adopted him as one of their own. Sir William Johnson then became known among them as *Warraghiyagey*, "one who does much business."

A bit of an upstart, William favored his own way of doing things over that of his uncle, over time acquiring much land in the valley. Deeply fascinated with Indian culture, William learned the language and dressed in their fashion, much to his uncle's chagrin. Still, his uncle could not deny William's success with the natives. Following the French and Indian War, the Mohawks gifted Johnson with over eighty thousand acres of native land, often measured simply by "as far as the eye can see" or "a man can walk in a day." Then, after living at his trading post, Fort Johnson, for many years, Sir William finally built a fine Mohawk Valley home: Johnson Hall, located farther north of the river outside Johnstown, New York. This stately valley home was the site of many conferences with the Iroquois, who camped on its lawn. Natives and white men frequently mingled about the house on any given day.

Sir William Johnson was instrumental in the early development of the Mohawk Valley and its economic success. He witnessed the rumblings of the War of Independence, and his influence helped keep the valley peaceful during those early days. However, he died unexpectedly at his home during an Indian conference on July 11, 1774. Sir William leaves us with only our imaginations about what his activity might have been during the Revolutionary War if he had lived. We can guess he would have fought against his rebellious neighbors. After all, he was a man of opportunity, Loyalist and brother to the Mohawks. His legacy lives on at the sites of Johnstown (named for his son), Fort Johnson and Johnson Hall.

Others of his family and friends became "enemies" among the Americans. Their names were barely whispered without disdain. Even William's son, John Johnson, who had been major general of the Tryon County Militia, was among those who fled to Canada when the war started.

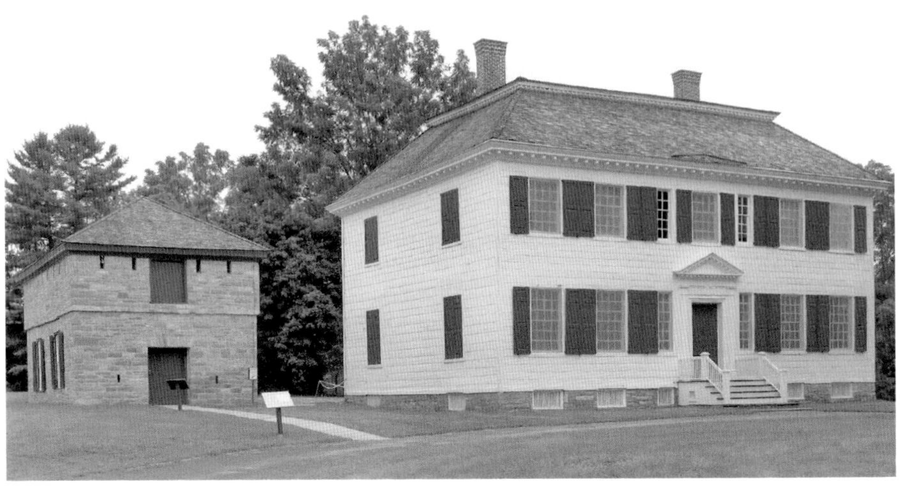

Johnson Hall, home of Sir William Johnson. *Courtesy of the author.*

John's only crime was his political support of the British. Americans feared he would influence the Indians, as did his father. As it turned out, however, the threat of influence came not from a man as much as from a woman; it came from William Johnson's wife, Molly. She and her brother, war chief Joseph Brant, became driving forces among the Iroquois who allied to the British. Of the Six Nations (Seneca, Cayuga, Onondaga, Oneida, Mohawk and Tuscarora), only the Oneidas and Tuscaroras remained steadfast in supporting the Americans.

Molly Brant: Mohawk Clan Mother and "Baroness"

One contributing factor to the division between the Indians and white settlers was their differing view of women's roles. Among the whites, a woman's place was at home; she raised the children, looked after household affairs and followed her husband. Colonists had a difficult time understanding that the Iroquois lived in a matriarchal society where family lineage followed that of the mother, not the father. The husband lived with his wife's family, hunting while the woman controlled the agriculture; in some cases, the wife fought beside her husband, though this was an exception. Native women sat at the council fires and chose clan chiefs. They controlled food supply and could sway decisions on making war. This was quite shocking for colonists, whose women never had a formal voice in politics. This separation of ideologies only added more mystery to the visage of Molly Brant, a fervent voice among her people. Molly Brant was a "women of two worlds."*

By the time of Molly's birth in about 1736, many natives of the Mohawk Valley had been Christianized, Molly's parents among them. Molly, sometimes called Mary, was born in the native village of Canajoharie on Route 5S, also called Indian Castle or Upper Mohawk Castle. However, as with so much of the unwritten history of the day, confusion exists about the actual location of her birth. The Canajoharie of her people is said to be different from the current-day village of Canajoharie. Some also suggest she was born in Ohio because her parents lived, for a time, along the Ohio River. We do know that after Molly's father, Peter, died, her mother returned to Canajoharie and married Nickus Brant, whom some historians believe to have been a sachem (chief) under a European name. Molly and her younger brother, Joseph, took the Brant name. Molly lived in her stepfather's house until her early twenties, contrary to the Indian way. Beyond this, both Molly and Joseph's early lives remain enigmatic. Uncertainty persists about whom Joseph's actual father might have been, though this mattered little among Indian peoples. The mother's line is what counted.

Well educated at a British mission school, able to read and write in English, Molly made a suitable match for Sir William Johnson when his first "wife" died. Sir William might have "sowed his seeds" many times before he settled down with Molly Brant. Some say he had at least one hundred illegitimate children. There was no stigma for such things during his time, as long as he could afford it. Other historians claim this is just a wild tale. We do know that William's first wife by common-law was his Johnson Hall German housekeeper, Catherine Weisenberg. She had been a runaway indentured servant, making her an unsuitable legal wife. In Molly, however, many believe Johnson found his soul mate. Even then, there is no record of an official wedding.

Molly was no stranger to politics when she "married" the general. At age eighteen, already a clan mother (voice among women), she accompanied a delegation of Mohawks to Philadelphia when they filed a complaint about

---

*. As with all stories and information used in this book, several resources and variations have been used to create them. In the case of early history, we must rely on a combination of stories and common knowledge. For indigenous peoples who had no written language, much of the information will come from nonindigenous sources, and this is always taken into consideration. One source for the Molly Brant story was the following: http://www.carf.info/kingston-past/molly-brant.

dishonest land dealings. From the native perspective, William Johnson made a suitable match for Molly, too. He was a wealthy, powerful conduit for negotiation to help the Indians get what they needed. In many ways, William and Molly were royalty.

Molly, many years younger than William, gave birth to their first child at age twenty-three. They had eight children altogether. Although not married in European terms, William named all of Molly's children in his will. Molly lived at both Fort Johnson and, later, Johnson Hall, where she played the role of grand dame very well. She was every bit a gentlewoman and mistress of her household, contradicting colonial views that Indians were uncouth and savage. Schooling and early association with white settlers had prepared her. She was described as being handsome and mannerly. Molly was William's right hand, perhaps even taking over control of her husband's duties regarding Indian affairs in his absence.

Molly had learned white women's housekeeping tasks even though William had servants and "Negro" slaves. Her role as lady of the house, or "housekeeper," as Williams referred to her in his writings, was a position of high esteem. Molly was a presence. One account stated, "One word from her goes farther than a thousand from any white man."

John Johnson, son of William and Catherine Weisenberg, took over as "lord of the manor" upon William's death. Molly retired with her children to Canajoharie, where she continued her husband's legacy as a trader until his estate was settled. William's other family members left for Canada in the early summer of 1775.

The Iroquois' decision of whether to support the Americans or British was not immediate, though some did choose sides quickly. Molly's brother Joseph attempted to convince them to break their treaty with the Americans, getting his wish in 1777. Molly's own activities included giving aid by way of supplies, food, shelter and information to Loyalists.

John Johnson later joined the remaining Johnsons and Butlers in Canada, as did Molly, though she might have bided her time in the valley acting as an unofficial British spy for a short span of time. A marker on Route 5 indicates a road leading to a house where she lived. Just exactly how she came to be there or at what time is uncertain. With a clear view of the river and roads, it might have been from here that Molly sent information to the British. It was because of her warning to the British that the Tyron County Militia was ambushed at Oriskany.

The mistress of Johnson Hall, now penniless except for what she earned in trade, left behind everything, home and land, right down to her beautiful silk

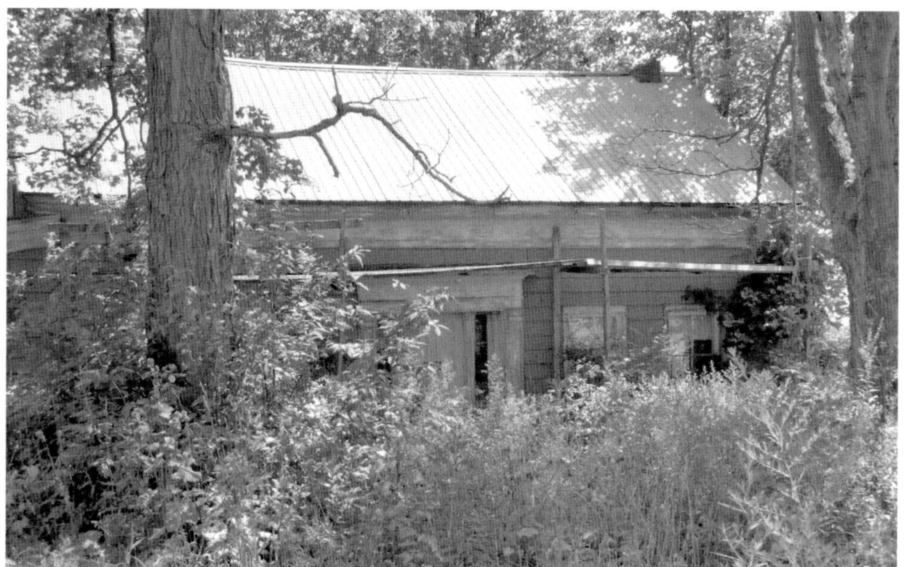

Late home of Molly Brant. She likely spied on the American Patriots from this location. *Courtesy of the author.*

gowns. She joined thousands of Mohawks as they traveled over two hundred miles to British-held Fort Niagara in Western New York, many starving and ill. Molly spent some time living in a house at the fort and then, in 1779, moved to a home on Carleton Island on the St. Lawrence River near Watertown, New York. She lost her seventeen-year-old son in the war. Her other children attended school in Montreal. Following the war, Molly's family took up residence in yet another house built for them in Kingston, Ontario. The British gave her a pension and compensation for her lost property.

As with many historical accounts, new information occasionally comes to light. It is suggested that Molly might actually have shunned the white man's culture, continuing to dress as an Indian and speak her native language and insisting that her children do the same. We do not know if this was during her time with Sir William Johnson, following his death or after the Revolutionary War. Whether this is the case or not, writings by her white contemporaries say otherwise.

Molly, a formidable figure, a rare woman, admired by the Mohawks and the British alike, born in the Mohawk Valley, died in Kingston, Ontario, in 1796. She was laid to rest as a Christian in what is now Saint Paul's churchyard. At the time of this book's publication, her actual grave site remains unknown.

The native way of life was eroding. Assimilation into the white American culture followed the war. The roles of native women changed with mixed marriages. Only the Oneidas and Tuscaroras, who sided with the Patriots, were granted reservation lands in the Mohawk Valley, though many chose to join their brethren in Canada.

German Palatines

The German Palatines originated in the Rhine's Electoral Palatinate. This was the historical territory of the Holy Roman Empire ruled by princes who represented the church. Near the end of the seventeenth century and into the early eighteenth century, it fell under constant attack from the French. Although once wealthy, monies had to be redirected to pay for military protection, leaving the region depleted and cast into famine. Many of these poor Protestants did what indigent peoples have done throughout history—they migrated elsewhere. In the case of the German Palatines, it was to England, where the government was sympathetic and promised free land in its American colonies.

The Palatines found themselves in the midst of debate. While many had hoped for passage to America, the British plan was to settle most in the British Isles. However, there were too many for England to handle, so in 1710, three thousand German Palatines sailed for the colonies. Most were forced into labor in order to pay for their passage. Though many remained in the Hudson Valley, in 1723, more than one hundred families were sent to the Mohawk Valley wilderness. These settlers spread throughout the region. One of the earliest settlements they founded was later called Palatine Bridge when a bridge was built over the Mohawk River. The Palatines also founded German Flatts. The region where they settled is commonly known as the Palatine District.

Having been forced from their homeland by extreme poverty and prejudice, thrown into badly supplied English migrant camps, carried thousands of miles over rough seas in disease-laden ships and then forced into servitude, what else could these hardworking Germans do? They turned their new freedom into success, thriving as farmers in the Mohawk Valley. The Palatine Germans lived as congenial neighbors to the Oneida Indians and the already established English, but the Revolution changed everything.

THE REVOLUTIONARY WAR ENTERS THE PEACEFUL MOHAWK VALLEY

Europeans were gradually settling wilderness areas west of Albany, especially along the fertile Mohawk River, already richly populated by natives of the Iroquois Confederacy. Land grants from King George of England to his loyal subjects gave birth to many homesteads and estates. The Mohawk Valley had escaped major ravaging during the French and Indian War, with only a few Indian raids, but the rumblings of revolution in the colonies was about to bring a new war into the peaceful valley. As such, an ideological rift pitted neighbor against neighbor. It became dangerous even to speak one's mind openly.

The British considered American Patriots to be traitors, while the Americans called those loyal to the king Tories. Many of these people who became enemies lived side by side. Growing tension forced some settlers to leave, while others built palisaded walls around their homes, making them forts unto themselves. The settlers' movements were watched with suspicious eyes for signs of sedition and treachery. Gone was the peaceful coexistence of Mohawk Valley residents.

It was late summer to early autumn in the valley, cradled in the rolling foothills of the northern Appalachian, Catskill and Adirondack Mountains. Fertile soil nourished crops needed by settlers, local militias and the Continental army. The harvest wasn't complete, but neat stacks of wheat stood like shadowy sentinels in the pre-dawn hours. Already, children stirred in their beds, while farmers with axes, horses and plows took to the fields. Wives banked fires and prepared breakfast or readied themselves to join their husbands in work.

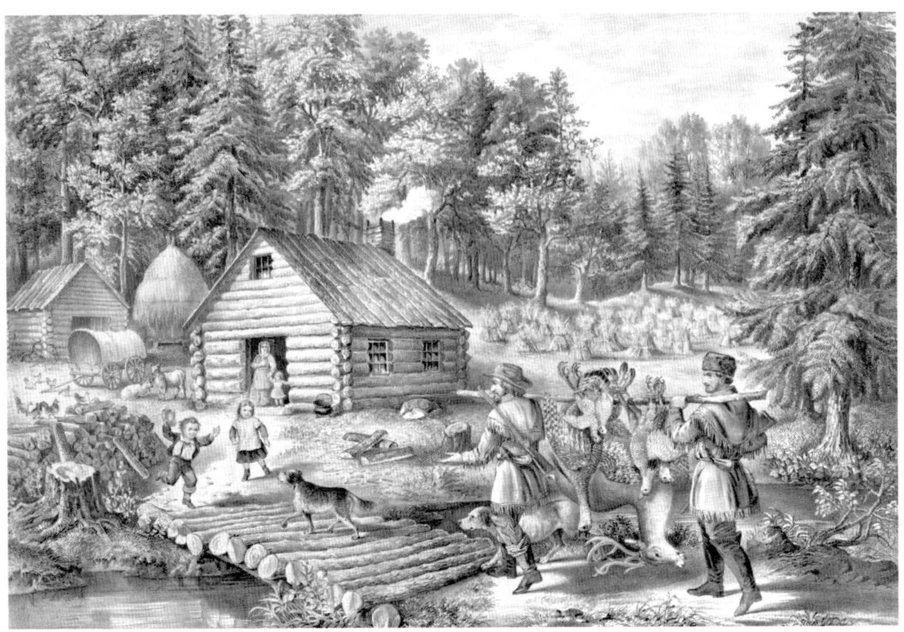

The pioneer's home on the western frontier. *Courtesy of the Library of Congress, Prints and Photographs Division.*

A frontier life meant being ready for long, cold winters in New York State. Time was precious. Nothing was wasted. Though drums of war echoed off mountaintops, the valley went about its life, unaware that a battle was on its way that would change everything. British General St. Leger was on the march, and every man from every Patriot home would be needed to stop him.

St. Leger and the Siege of Fort Schuyler

The British built Fort Stanwix in 1758 at what is today Rome, New York. The fort protected them from the French and guarded the head of the Mohawk River and Wood Creek confluence. This portage used for centuries by natives was called the Oneida Carry for that reason. The waterway led north to Lake Ontario, which gave the British easy access to Canada. When it no longer served them, the fort fell into disrepair.

Farsighted Americans, seeing its significance, rebuilt and manned the fort in June 1776. Because Stanwix was the name of a British general, Patriots changed the name to honor one of their leaders, General Philip Schuyler. The name later reverted back to Fort Stanwix, perhaps because of a second Fort Schuyler in nearby Utica or because of titles given to various treaties using the name Fort Stanwix. It served the Continental army as a major point of defense against its founders.

Fort Schuyler was put to the test in the summer of 1777. Had the Americans correctly assessed the fort's importance? Yes! British colonel Barry St. Leger found it daunting enough to lay siege to it. That onslaught lasted from August 2 to August 22. While Leger expected the Continental army stationed under command of Peter Gansevoort to surrender to his "superior" forces, his plans never came to fruition.

Tyron County Militia and Scout Lieutenant (Johan) Adam Helmer

The Tyron County Militia was formed, like many of its kind, to protect early settlements. It guarded most of the Mohawk Valley. Prior to the Revolution, these militias were enforcers for various committees of safety. Many such committees were formed in the 1760s, serving as local governments. Made up of all adult males in a community, they looked after the concerns of their populace. These committees also included groups of "able-bodied men" or local militia that acted under direction of the committee at large. The Tryon County Committee of Safety was formed on August 27, 1774. In 1776, its purpose changed to that of carrying out orders for the Continental Congress. Tryon County's most renowned militiaman, made even more famous by Walter D. Edmonds's 1936 novel, *Drums Along the Mohawk*, was scout Johan Adam Helmer. Edmonds's book was later made into a movie starring Henry Fonda and Claudette Colbert, though historical facts were changed for the movie, as often happens.

Known commonly as Adam, this twenty-four-year-old farmer with a young wife and son was already a veteran of war before his famed run of 1778. A scout in the Tyron County Militia under Brigadier General Herkimer, Adam and two others were dispatched to Fort Schuyler (Fort Stanwix, Rome, New York) from Fort Dayton (Herkimer) near Adam's home in the Mohawk Valley. Their message for Colonel Peter Gansevoort in command there was plain: "British forces planned a siege on the fort." In the meantime, the remaining Tyron militia, approximately eight hundred men including Adam's father and brother, marched toward Fort Schuyler. The militia intended to head off the British moving south from Oswego under Lieutenant Colonel St. Leger, who was on his way to join Burgoyne's army on the Hudson near Albany. Fort Schuyler blocked Leger's way. The militia never made it to the fort.

Tired from their thirty-mile trek, which began on August 4 through forests on a poor military road, General Herkimer's Tyron County Militia arrived at the top of a ravine near Oriskany, New York. It was August 6, 1777, when the general ordered his troops into the heavily treed ravine to continue their march toward the fort. No doubt, pushing his men angered Herkimer, as it had not been his plan to force this early attack against Leger. He was pressured by allegations that he delayed sending reinforcements to Fort Schuyler because he was a Tory. Those were indeed "fighting words" to such an honorable man.

Unknown to the Patriots, Joseph Brant's sister Molly, wife of Loyalist Sir William Johnson, sent a warning to St. Leger. Leger then sent a force made up of his allies. They included Tories from the valley, with Joseph Brant's Indians, Butler's rangers and troops under the command of Sir William Johnson's son John. Their orders were to halt Herkimer. In effect, many were local men—neighbors of those in the Tyron County Militia—bringing home again the tragedy that befell the beautiful landscape. Blood was spilled not by strangers but often by neighboring farmers.

Brant's raiders took up positions in the ravine and on the opposite crest of the hill, waiting in ambush. Herkimer's Patriots were indeed surprised as musket fire broke through their column on three sides.

Herkimer took a shot in the leg that toppled his mount. He was brought to the hilltop, opposite Brant's raiding party. The general sat smoking his pipe beneath a shade tree, calling out orders to his men even as he bled into the earth. Though courageous, the small militia could do little more than hold its own, suffering heavy casualties. British forces took their fair share of damage, too, which would lead to their eventual retreat. The militia's losses were not in vain.

Wounded militiamen limped back into the valley to what safety their forts and homes could offer. It was a terrible moment for Tyron County, taking the life of a much-beloved general. Herkimer's leg could not be saved. He died in his home from a botched amputation about ten days later.

The siege on the fort had already begun by the time Herkimer entered that ravine. The only saving grace was that Adam Helmer made it to Fort

Schuyler. The Battle of Oriskany was considered a draw, even though the militia weakened the British enough to make a difference.

British troops were forced to retreat when Gansevoort refused to surrender the fort. Furthermore, the Americans rallied when word came that Benedict Arnold had arrived at Fort Dayton with reinforcements. Yet the beating taken by the Tyron County Militia unsettled the valley, making known its vulnerability. In addition to the sorrows of many households who suffered loss at Oriskany, Adam Helmer lost both his father and his brother but never his courage—that would save many lives in German Flatts one year later.

Burning of German Flatts and Adam's Run

A year had passed since British general John Burgoyne was defeated at Saratoga, ending his attempt to split the colonies. Still, the British army, with its professional soldiers and allies, held its own. Well supplied by way of Quebec, it managed the winter of 1777 far better than the "upstart" Patriots. Yet the Mohawk Valley was a problem for the British. Stalwart even after heavy casualties at Oriskany, farmers continued to supply Washington's army.

Joseph Brant, along with other British-allied Indians, developed plans to block shipments of food and men from the valley. From his village base of Onaquaga (Windsor, New York), Brant led raiding parties throughout the valley, beginning in May 1778. His Indians ravaged many settlements throughout that summer. Crops and other property were destroyed and many captives taken.

While well protected by its militia, the region was not prepared to handle scattered assaults. These farmers and merchants were trained at local forts in tactics used by the regular army, but Indians raided and disappeared before militias could respond. Incursions by troops on Indian villages and by Indians on white settlements became a matter of tit-for-tat retaliation. Brant swooped into the Mohawk Valley with a contingent of Butler's Rangers, and they were not alone. They had with them British regulars, Tories and Indians.

On September 16, 1778, the valley skies danced red with the glow of flames.

Adam Helmer was once more called upon to scout for the Continental army. This time, he and eight others set out to Unadilla Valley, forty to sixty miles southward from current Route 5. Reports were that Joseph Brant and his forces had set up camps along the Susquehanna River. Helmer's scouts

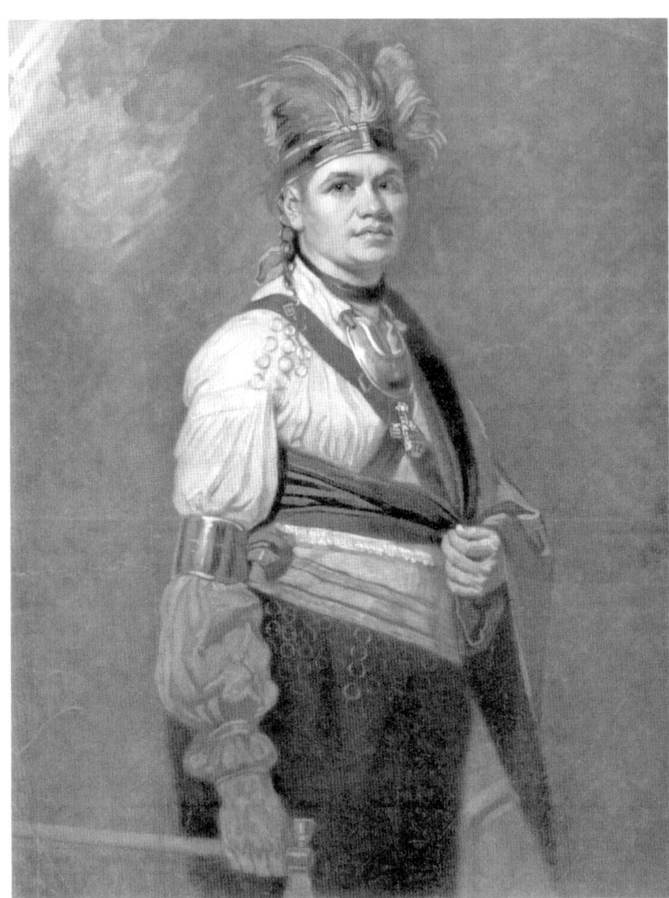

Left: Joseph Fayadaneega, called Brant, the "Great Captain of the Six Nations." *Courtesy of the Library of Congress, Prints and Photographs Division.*

Below: A bank note illustration showing colonists praying for deliverance from imminent Indian attack. *Courtesy of the Library of Congress, Prints and Photographs Division.*

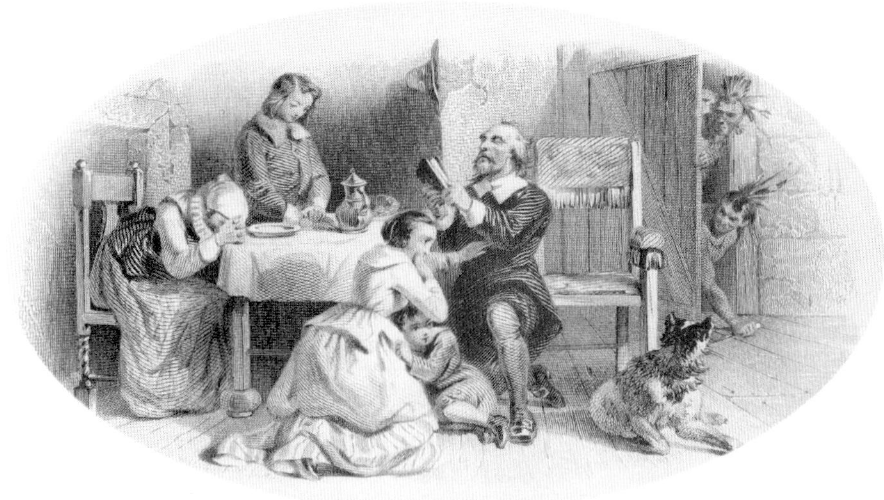

were to gather information and determine whether Brant was a threat to winter stores in the Mohawk region.

Edmeston, New York, lies approximately halfway from Fort Dayton to Unadilla. It was there, near Carr Farm, that Helmer's scouts were set upon by some of Brant's men. As before, it was only Adam Helmer who escaped this attack. So began his famous run.

It is truly hard to imagine what a man is thinking in the split seconds that mean the difference between life and death—or worse, torture. Yet Adam had the wherewithal to devise a plan of action even as his feet took flight. Accounts of his run say he ran first toward Andrustown (Jordanville, New York) to warn his sister's family that Brant was coming. Here he was given new shoes to wear. Onward he ran to Columbia and Petries Corners, where settlers fled to Fort Dayton. By the time Adam himself arrived at the fort, he was badly cut and bruised from his run. Regardless, he made his report to Colonel Bellinger: at least two hundred British and Indians were on their way to the Mohawk Valley, and they were bent on destruction, with the notorious Captain William Caldwell among them leading his company of rangers.

Adam Helmer ran from Carr Farm in Edmeston to Fort Dayton, many more than the thirty miles on today's maps when one considers thick underbrush, fallen trees, rocks and hills. This feat was incredible.

Even with most settlers sheltered in nearby forts, more than sixty valley homesteads were set on fire along with their barns filled with harvest.

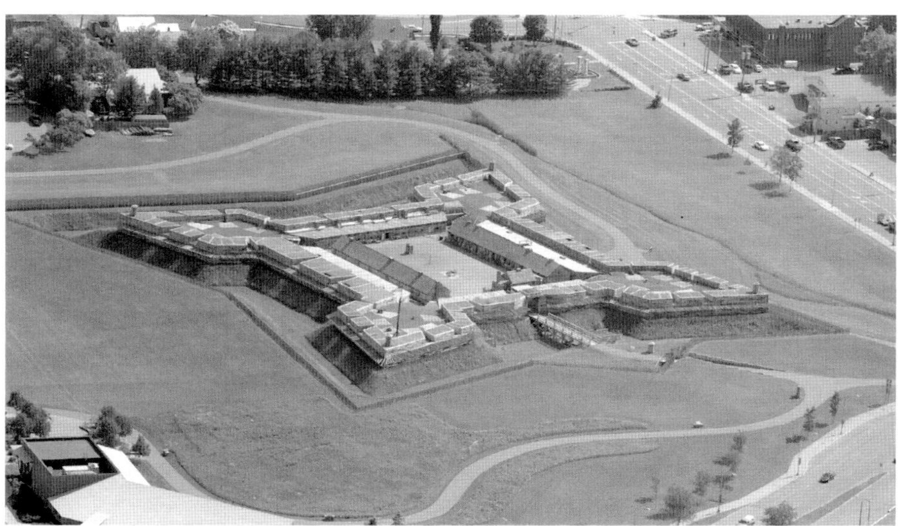

Fort Stanwix, aerial view. *Courtesy of John Clifford and the* Rome Sentinel.

Over eight hundred head of livestock were killed or taken. The marauders destroyed crops and property on both sides of the river, including mills that processed grain into flour. Loss of human life was little to none thanks to Adam Helmer's great courage, together with his stamina and perhaps an abundant helping of good fortune.

To this day, only three of the other scouts who set out with Adam have been found. These bodies were later buried at Carr Farm. The rest remain a mystery. They might have been taken captive, dying elsewhere.

Whether raids in the Mohawk Valley were retaliations or planned efforts to wipe out a major grain supply remains a topic of discussion. The lasting affect is undeniable. Following the burning of German Flatts, seven hundred people were left homeless. The Mohawk Valley's population dropped from ten thousand to only three thousand between 1777 and 1781. With the violence and harsh weather, many residents did not survive, while others moved away.

Loyalists were no longer welcome. Many—like the Johnsons, Brants and Butlers—fled to Canada, some at the start of the war and some after American victory. The Americans held John Butler's wife prisoner in Albany until the war ended.

Events can so drastically change an environment. Perhaps if grain had continued uninterrupted as a major crop throughout the war or herds of livestock increased, villages of the valley might be much larger communities today. Instead, most rely on small industry and tourism.

"Nefarious" Butlers

Rangers were the British answer to the American militia. Most famous or infamous among the companies were Roger's Rangers, formed by Robert Rogers during the French and Indian War. But for much of the Revolutionary War, the valley feared Butler's Rangers, led by John Butler and his son Walter.

John Butler was not only a good friend to William Johnson, but he was also Johnson's successful Indian interpreter. He later served as a military captain in Johnson's service and was a staunch Loyalist, second in wealth in the Mohawk Valley only to Johnson. His five-thousand-acre estate, Butlersbury, stood on Switzer Hill near Fonda, New York, within full view of the Mohawk River. Even his father had been in service to Britain. It was Walter Butler Sr., one-time commander at Fort Hunter, who procured this estate for him.

John's son Walter was born in 1752 near Johnstown, New York, also called Kalaneka, on Indian land. Walter had a law practice in Albany. Ironically, when war positioned neighbor against neighbor, many of Walter Butler's previous legal clients found themselves in opposition to their lawyer. Very little else is known of Walter Butler's private life, perhaps because he was a young man on the cusp of making his own way when the Butlers were forced to move from the valley.

During the war years, Walter Butler was in service to the king as an ensign in the Eighth Regiment. He fought at the Battle of Oriskany, later joining his father's rangers as a captain. After being captured by Patriots at Shoemaker's Tavern in German Flatts, Walter Butler was sent to prison in Albany. He was there for only a few months when he escaped to Canada. He returned later to be involved in raids against settlements. However, on October 30, 1781, while fleeing with his rangers from another raid in the Mohawk Valley, Walter Butler was slain. The very man responsible for his earlier imprisonment, Lieutenant Colonel Marinus Willet, sent his Oneida Indian allies in pursuit. Accounts vary, with many legends growing over the years, about what happened at the ford of West Canada Creek, which today forms a natural border between Herkimer and Oneida Counties. One such account states that many of Butler's men were killed or captured by the Oneidas. Walter Butler rode his horse into shallow waters, dismounted and tried to run into the brush but then turned, shouting, "Shoot and be damned!" At that moment, one of the Indians shot Butler through the head with a musket ball. Some say the Oneida's name was Lewey (Louey), who took the scalp and also had a fine ranger's coat after that day. One report claims the Indians cried, "Butler for Cherry Valley!"

Opinions of the Butlers would depend on which side you found yourself during the war. They were heroes to the British, though it might be argued that even the British found their tactics uncomfortable, to say the least. To Patriots, they were the most hated murderers. Their departure was reason for celebration, not sorrow. John Butler was forever labeled with the massacres in Wyoming, Pennsylvania, and Walter was given the distinction of owning the Cherry Valley Massacre. In Walter's defense, he was a good leader, holding back long enough to allow his men to escape across the creek.

Cherry Valley Massacre

Troubles in the Mohawk Valley were centered on what we now call Route 5, but Route 20 was not without its share of Revolutionary War activity. Route 20 was also a major east–west passage, though instead of following a river, it followed the natural curvature in the Catskill foothills. About forty miles of rugged, forested landscape lay between Route 5 at German Flatts and Route 20 at Cherry Valley.

Failures by the British at Forts Schuyler and Saratoga, the burning of German Flatts and the Wyoming Massacre, set off a raging blaze that swept through Indian villages and white settlements alike.

Cherry Valley was a small but significant village with a newly built stockade fort nestled in the Catskill foothills. Like German Flatts, it lay sleepily awaiting the descent of the cold winter months. Crops had been harvested and stored before that fateful November 11, 1778, when something more sinister than any New York State winter gripped the settlement. It is said to be the bloodiest, most horrific massacre of the Revolutionary War. Walter Butler's loss of control over his native allies led to the brutal murders of not only armed defenders but also at least thirty unarmed men, women and children. The region had never seen such horror, nor would it ever again.

British-allied Indians set up bases in a handful of native villages, including Unadilla and Onaquaga. Neither of these major Indian sites lies along Routes 5 and 20, but they directly effect what happened at Cherry Valley. Following the Mohawk Valley's devastation, Continental troops rallied to root out raiding bands formed by Brant and Butler and struck at their heart.

Unadilla, translated as "Meeting Place," had two villages—a white settlement that began around 1770 and an Indian village. Loyalists were using both, so Patriot forces destroyed them. Onaquaga was a large Indian village and Joseph Brant's base. It was from here that he plotted raids, including the one on German Flatts. This, too, was annihilated.

Many believe the massacre at Cherry Valley was retaliation for what happened in these native villages. Some historians also believe that although British Loyalists joined the attack that day, their Indian allies were particularly brutal, angered by accusations that they were to blame for what happened at Wyoming. Furthermore, the Indians were bitter over Walter Butler's poor treatment of Joseph Brant following Wyoming, even though Brant was supposedly not present in Pennsylvania.

In the eighteenth century, the enemy would be little threat during winter months because it was hunting season. Snowfall in October and the presence

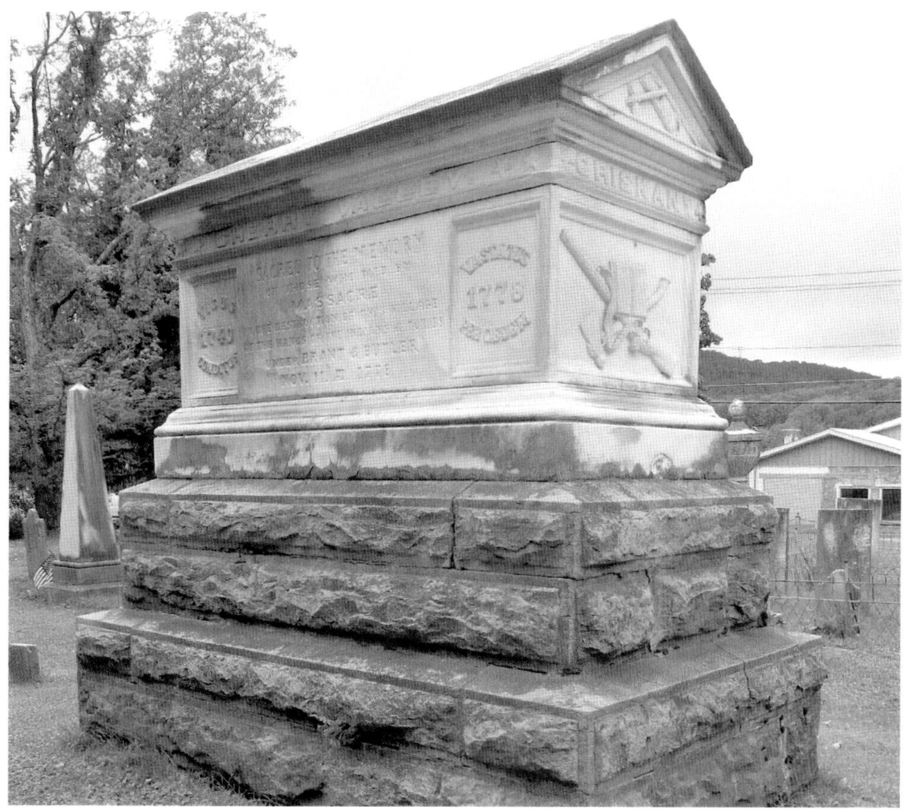

Cherry Valley Massacre mass grave. *Courtesy of the author.*

of Continental soldiers allowed inhabitants to relax and begin the process of settling in for cold weather. Prior to Colonel Alden's arrival earlier that summer, settlers had been on high alert all the time. Now in the shadow of Fort Alden, they moved back into their homes. Then on November 8, word arrived of a possible attack.

A message from Fort Schuyler warned Colonel Ichabod Alden of impeding danger, which he stubbornly ignored. As with many militarily trained officers, Alden was unfamiliar with frontier methods used by Indians and made only rudimentary preparations in advance of the onslaught. The colonel determined the news to be just another of many such rumors. After all, his scouts had reported no real action in his region. The people begged to be allowed to store up food and take shelter in the fort. Believing it a waste of time, Alden refused them. Instead, he gave orders to secure the fort and retired to his quarters outside the walls, as did his officers.

Alden sent an additional scouting party to search for signs of trouble, if only to cover his refusal to the villagers. Those scouts never returned with the warning but woke on the morning of November 10 as prisoners of Captain Butler. It was only a short time until Butler learned from the scouts that officers of Fort Alden were comfortably housed outside its stockade. Alden's lack of action was a mortal mistake.

A snowfall added to what already covered the ground. It turned to rain in the early hours of November 11 as fog shrouded the valley. Nobody, not even the soldiers, wished to wander out into *that* weather. A little longer by the warm fire could do no harm, or so they might have thought. Anyone living in these regions knows the feeling on a chill winter morning. Roll over, pull up the covers, go back to sleep. Soldiers did not have the luxury of sleeping in, nor did most anyone living in those difficult times. Yet home was warmer than the quarter-mile walk to the fort, so they whiled away the morning.

Musket fire rent the peaceful silence around noon. Five to six hundred British and Indians swarmed into the village, killing Alden as he attempted to reach the fort and killing or capturing the other officers. The fort was missing its leadership in the blink of an eye.

The fort's cannons answered the attack with an immediate volley. There were not enough soldiers left within the fort to venture beyond its walls. These men were helpless to do anything but watch and listen for the next thirty-six hours as Butler and Brant's forces killed, scalped and tortured innocent settlers, destroyed property and set fire to the village. Surely, that would weigh heavy on a man's conscience forever. Some inhabitants managed to escape into the forest, later making their way into the fort. During this time, those inside the fort were besieged.

Most of the dead were women and children. Another seventy or so women and children, with a handful of men, were taken captive. Over thirty homes and barns lay in ashes, along with two mills and a blacksmith shop. Food was taken or destroyed, along with livestock, leaving 180 or more settlers with no supplies, clothing or shelter to stave off the rest of the winter, which had only just begun. Forty or so of the inhabitants taken prisoner returned to the village four days later. This only added to the burden of caring for so many with so little.

Torturous snows continued to fall, becoming knee deep in places. Yet the fate of the captives from Cherry Valley was far worse. Later accounts from prisoners who escaped, were released or rescued stated that they were taken on a forced march some two hundred miles through winter

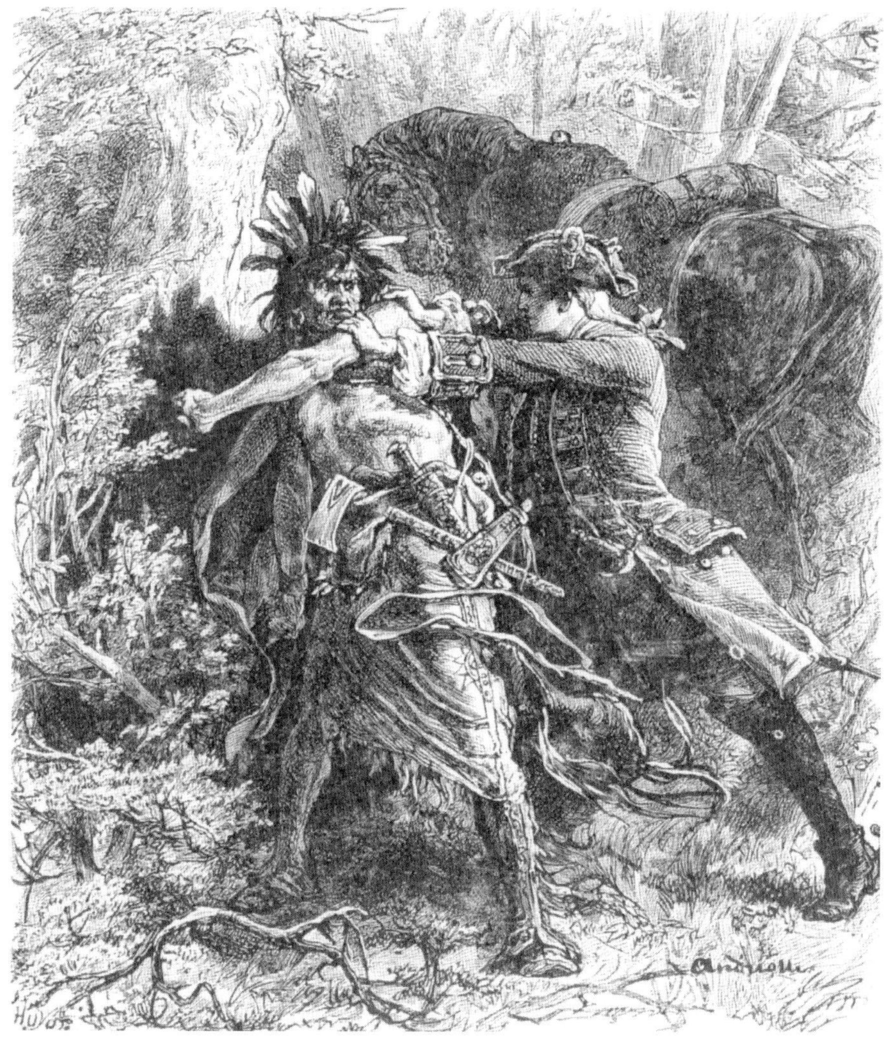

The struggle of a frontier militiaman with a Mohawk brave. *Courtesy of the Library of Congress, Prints and Photographs Division.*

snows until they reached the Indian village of Kanadaseago (Seneca Castle), near Geneva, New York.

The diary of one Captain Benjamin Warren, as researched by David E. Alexander,* highlights the horrors of those two days at Cherry Valley:

---

*. This is one excerpt from David Alexander's work. More can be found at the following: http://www.newrivernotes.com/historical_revolutionary_1778_cherry_hill_massacre_ny.htm.

November 13th. In the afternoon and morning of the 13th we sent out parties after the enemy withdrew; brought in the dead; such a shocking sight my eyes never beheld before of savage and brutal barbarity; to see the husband mourning over his dead wife with four dead children lying by her side, mangled, scalpt, and some their heads, some their legs and arms cut off, some torn the flesh off their bones by their dogs—12 of one family killed and four of them burnt in his house.

The Wyoming and Cherry Valley Massacres, along with the decimation of German Flatts, sparked a fighting fire in the hearts of American Patriots that would not go out until the war was won.

"Everyman's" Fortifications

The military built forts for housing its soldiers, but inhabitants of the valley also needed places of refuge during raids. For the most part, this meant a fortified homestead, meetinghouse or church. Several of these were found throughout the Mohawk Valley. Many times, the use of these fortifications overlapped between military base and residential shelter. They were part of a string of forts protecting the frontier.

Fort Paris in Stone Arabia was one such farm, though all that is left is a sign marking the Stone Arabia Battlefield. This is north off Route 5 on Route 10. The home once located at that site was built in 1737. A palisade enclosed the house, trading post and barracks for one hundred men. This is where Colonel John Brown's Americans were defeated on October 18, 1780.

Old Fort Herkimer, built in 1740, was on the river's south side opposite West Canada Creek. A map drawn in 1756 shows the two-story stone house surrounded by a palisade and six-foot trench, complete with bastions that did not commonly surround more simple fortifications of other homesteads. Known earlier as Fort Kaouri, it was demolished in 1825 to make way for the Erie Canal. It had been home to Johann Jost Herkimer (Herchhcimer), a wealthy Palatine landowner with over five thousand acres in the valley. Johann was the father of General Nicholas Herkimer, who had his first command at this fort during the French and Indian War. In 1757, when French and Indian forces attacked German Flatts, Johann gathered as many residents as he could shelter. Others were killed or taken prisoner.

Fortified Herkimer Home in Little Falls was the home of General Nicholas Herkimer. Today, it is a museum beside the Herkimer family cemetery and burial place of the general, who died following the Battle of Oriskany. One gets a sense of just how isolated these farmsteads were when standing in the yard.

Fort Herkimer's sister fort, Fort Dayton, named for its builder, Colonel Elias Dayton, was the destination of Adam Helmer's famous run. Benedict Arnold, a once brave man who later fell from grace, also served at Fort Dayton. Located on the north side of the river, it, too, housed settlers when needed. Fort Dayton markers are found in the center of Herkimer village. The early Herkimer settlement actually extended to both sides of the river, encompassing what are now Herkimer, Mohawk and Ilion.

Located on Route 5S, along the Mohawk River, is Fort Herkimer Church. This is east of Mohawk, New York, and south of Herkimer. Built in the mid-1700s by German Palatines during the French and Indian War, it is one of New York State's oldest churches and the oldest building in Herkimer County. This fort protected the valley in both the French and Indian and Revolutionary Wars. It was used mostly for colonial militia during

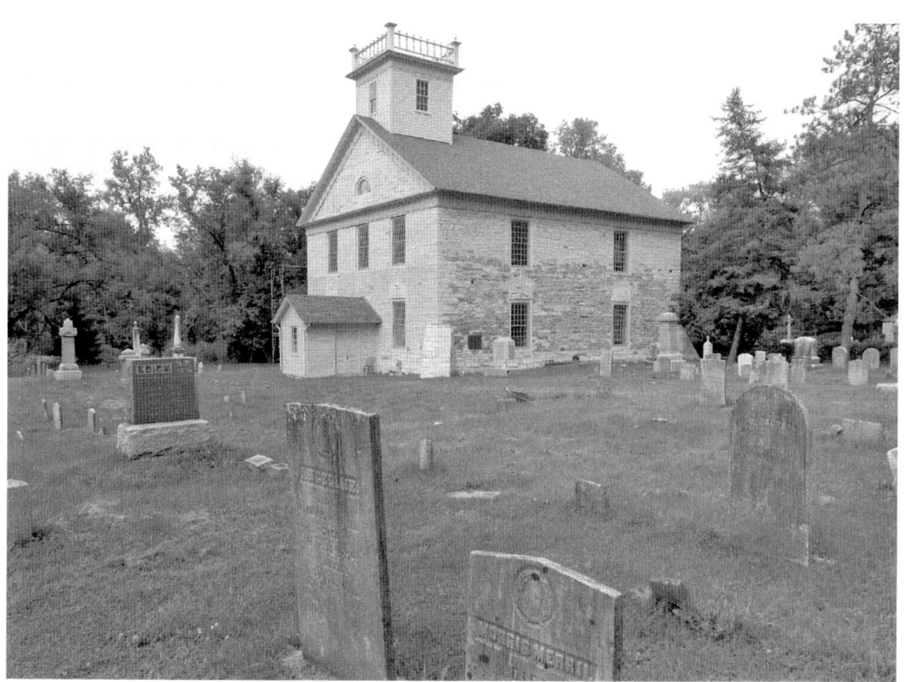

Fort Herkimer Church and burial site of Adam Helmer. *Courtesy of the author.*

the Revolution, though sometimes it harbored settlers. A stockade wall surrounded the limestone church that remains a place of worship today. Adam Helmer is buried in the church graveyard.

As previously discussed, the first home of Sir William Johnson served as a fort as well. Fort Johnson was a stately manor by comparison to other homes in the region, though plain compared to Johnson Hall. During the French and Indian War, it was not only home to William but also to his German common-law wife and to Molly Brant. After William built Johnson Hall, Fort Johnson became the home of his son John. Upon William's death, John inherited Johnson Hall. As was often true in times of war, the Commission of Safety forced John out, confiscating the Tory stronghold. What intrigue those walls must hold!

The most completely restored fortified homestead in the valley is beautiful Fort Klock, located on Route 5 just two miles east of St. Johnsville. Today, it is operated as a museum with events throughout the year. Many reenactments are held there in warmer months.

Fort Klock was the eighteenth-century home of Johannes Klock. Loopholes pierced two-foot-thick walls of the stone house so soldiers could shoot their rifles from inside; this was true of Fort Herkimer as well. Fort Klock was the site of one of the Revolutionary War's last battles, the Battle of Klock's Field, on October 19, 1780. John Johnson and Joseph Brant swept through the valley, meeting here with forces of General Robert Van Rensselaer. This battle ended what is sometimes called the Great Raid. Area residents flocked to the fort as Johnson and Brant set up battle lines nearby, effectively blockading the way to St. Johnsville. Van Rensselaer charged their position, scattering them quickly. Nonetheless, American losses were significant.

There is a museum now just below the site of Fort Plain. Although sometimes called Fort Plank, according to many historians, the forts were two distinct entities. Built by Colonel Dayton in 1776, it served as a refuge for residents. A scene from the movie *Drums Along the Mohawk* portrays a raid in which women donned soldiers' uniforms and took to the walls with muskets among the men. While women's roles included bringing water and food to soldiers, as well as tending the wounded, making ammunition and helping to load weapons, they seldom took an active role in battle. However, women did put on men's clothing in a battle at Fort Plain in 1780 in defense of a large force of Tories and Indians. Greatly outnumbered, the garrison risked falling, but the enemy retreated, believing it filled with worthy defenders. The women of the valley scored a victory for the Americans with their clever ruse.

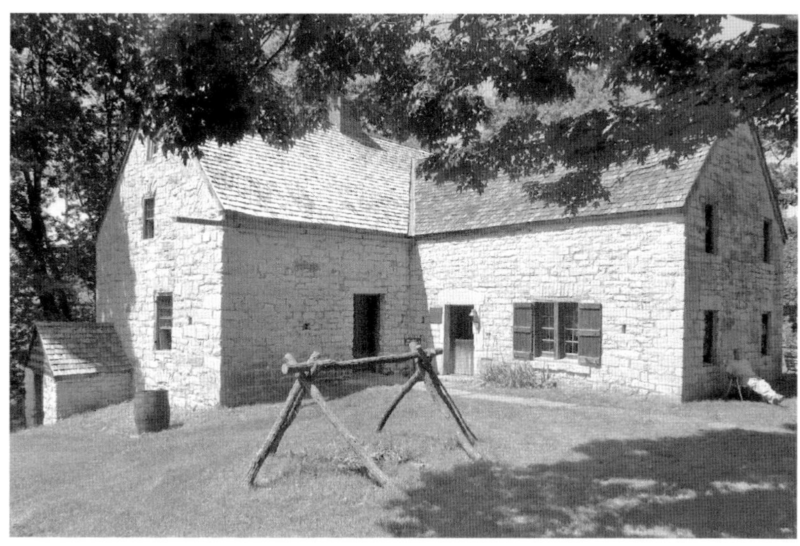

Fort Klock, fortified homestead. *Courtesy of the author.*

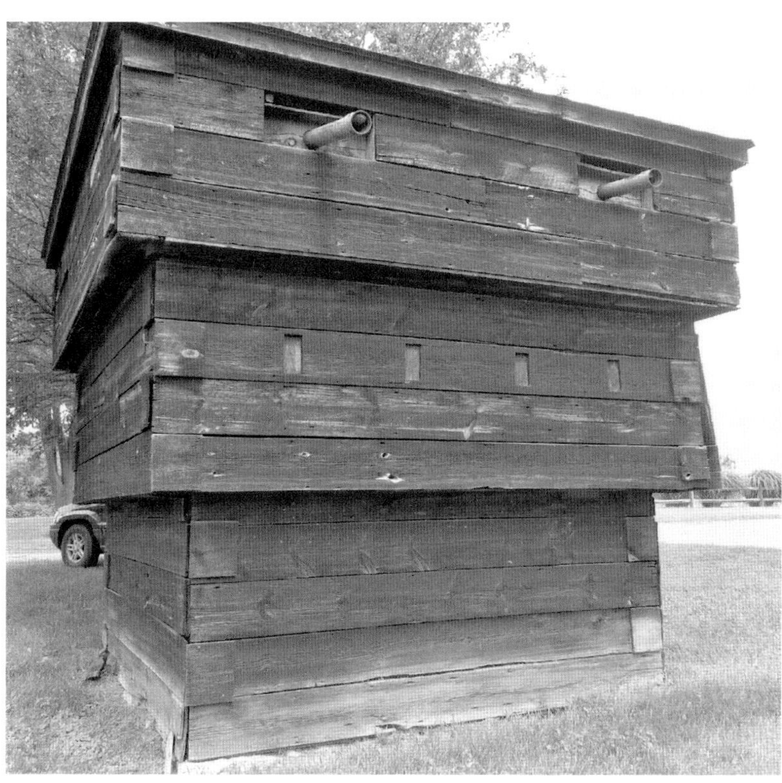

Blockhouse model, Fort Plain. *Courtesy of the author.*

Some of America's most famous Patriots came to Fort Plain. Van Rensselaer commanded the fort, as did the later mayor of New York City, Colonel Marinus Willett. It was even inspected by George Washington himself, who viewed many of the valley forts at this time, including Fort Dayton. From its location overlooking the valley, Patriots watched the roads within view of other nearby forts. Runners were sent throughout the valley with warnings of impending danger. Like most of the valley forts, Fort Plain exists as only a marker today.

A very early cabin, possibly pre-1700, built by Hendrick Frey, later served as an outpost or fort. It served the British as a palisaded fort until 1739, when it was replaced with a stone building with loopholed walls—a common makeover for many resident forts. This homestead served the British throughout the French and Indian War. Fort Frey, now a private residence, is located on Route 5.

The Frey family is a perfect example of how conflict often separated neighbors and, more tragically, family. Hendrick senior had three sons—Henry, John and Bernard. Henry was a Loyalist, so he was taken prisoner. Henry's property was seized during the War for Independence, and Fort Frey served the Patriots. Bernard, also a Loyalist, became a captain in Butler's

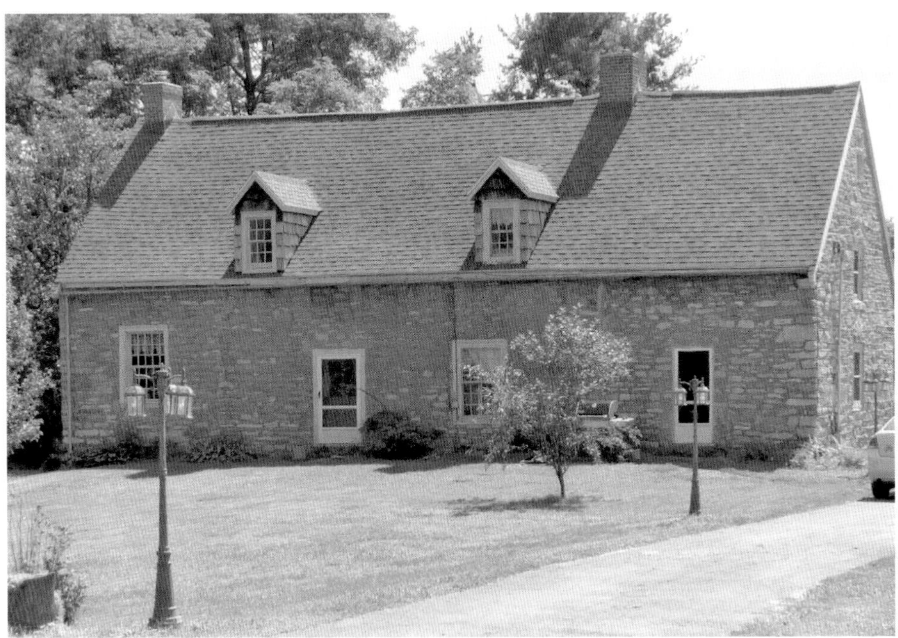

Fort Frey, private residence. *Courtesy of the author.*

Rangers. However, John, who was a friend of John Butler, joined the Patriots and became a major in the Tyron County Militia. He was taken prisoner during the Battle of Oriskany, although later released. In other words, friend was pitted against friend, brother against brother.

Fort Wagner was the 1750 farmstead of Johan Peter Wagner. Traveling on Route 5, one can see a marker and the house. He and his wife are buried in a family plot nearby. Their son, also Johan Peter, was a lieutenant colonel in the Continental army and was present at Oriskany. This home passed from father to son and down the family line. It is easy to distinguish the older from the newer section of this home. The house's stone section was the fortified addition.

There are quite a few Fort Hunters, including one in Albany County and another along the Susquehanna River in Pennsylvania. There was also a Fort Hunter in the Mohawk Valley. It was located near the native village of Tionontoguen (the Meeting of the Waters), currently the tiny town of Florida, New York, south of Amsterdam. This is the confluence of the Mohawk River and Schoharie Creek. Built by the British, as ordered by Queen Anne, to be a missionary outpost in 1711, the fort was named after colonial governor Robert Hunter. Unlike fortified homesteads, this was a military fort with blockhouses at each corner. A wooden chapel named for Queen Anne was built at its center in 1712 and then rebuilt in 1741 using local limestone. A series of articles collected by Leslie Devereux suggest that Fort Hunter enclosed thirty Mohawk cabins. Additional reports say that as many as six hundred Christianized Indians might have lived in or near the fort by 1775. The chapel was used after the War for Independence as a tavern and possibly a stable. The mission's decline was largely due to a Loyalist Mohawk congregation and English church leaders forced from the valley. The fort and chapel have now gone the way of Fort Herkimer, torn down for the Erie Canal.

The chapel at Fort Hunter founded today's Parish of Saint Ann in Amsterdam, New York. A legendary silver communion set gifted by Queen Anne is now said to be in use at the church in Brantford, Canada, where many Loyalists fled under the leadership of Joseph Brant.

The list of forts, both homestead and militarily built, is lengthy. It is safe to say that almost every larger home in the valley was a fort, especially if owned by a military leader. Most are now shadowy memories, grown over, built over, walked upon or lost. Fort Plain's site gives a complete overview of many of these fortifications.

Palatine Churches of the Valley

As with the homesteads, many churches in the Mohawk Valley also became wartime fortifications or, as with Queen Anne's Chapel, succumbed to the politics of war.

Beyond the missionaries who entered the valley with the "divine" goal of winning "heathen" souls, early white settlers were also people of religion. They found strength in their Christian faith during the most difficult of times. Most noteworthy of the churches in the valley are Old Palatine Church on Route 5 and the Trinity Lutheran and Reformed Dutch Churches of Stone Arabia, just north of Route 5 on Route 10.

Old Palatine Church was built in 1770 on land donated by Hendrick W. Nellis, a Loyalist who later fled to Canada. The church itself was founded much earlier, in 1749, but most likely, congregants met in homes or a common meetinghouse prior to it being built. Van Rensselaer's company camped here following the Battle of Klock's Field. Although all those who

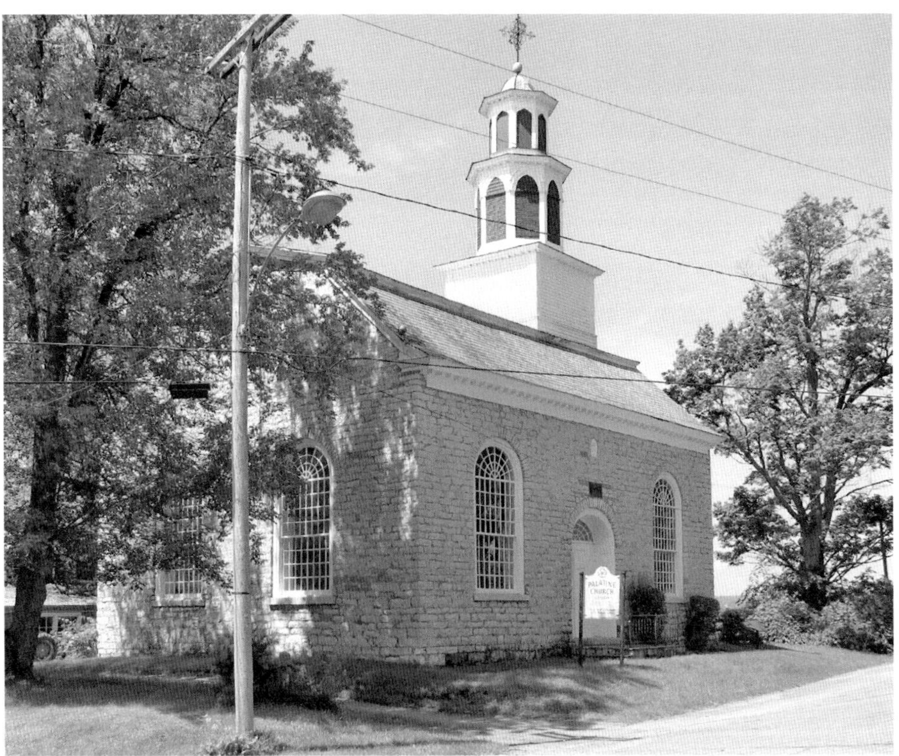

Old Palatine Church. *Courtesy of the author.*

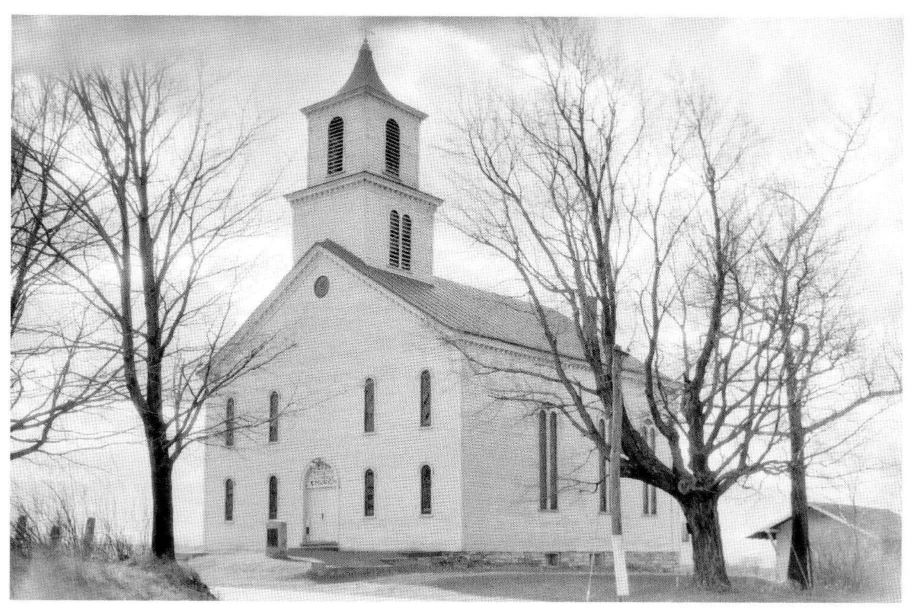

Trinity Lutheran Church, State Route 10, Stone Arabia, Montgomery County, New York. *Historic American Buildings Survey, Nelson E. Baldwin, photographer, August 5, 1936,* SOUTHWEST ELEVATION. *Courtesy of the Library of Congress, Prints and Photographs Division.*

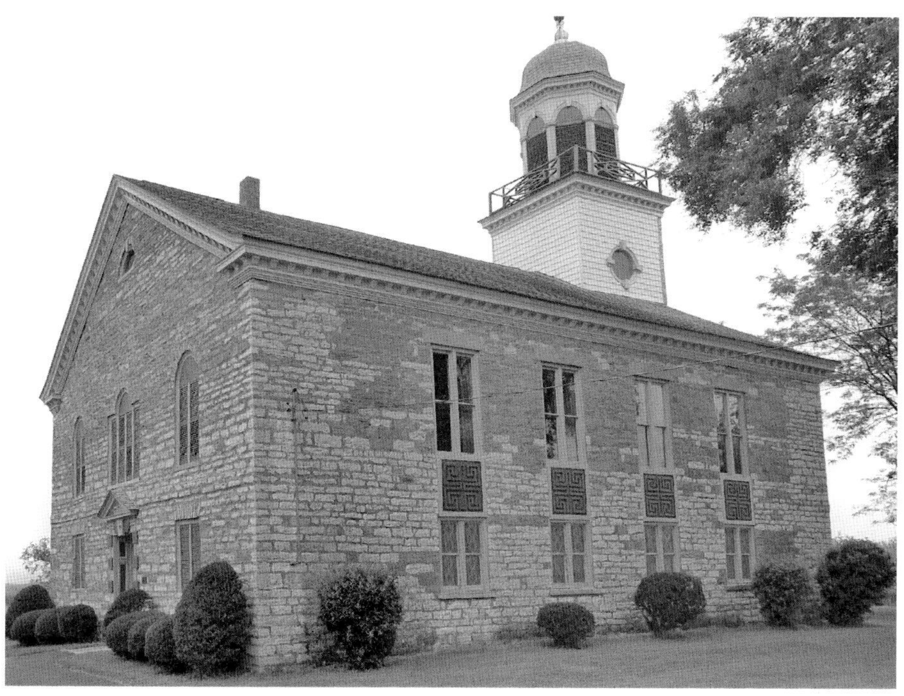

Reformed Dutch Church. *Courtesy of the author.*

remained loyal to Britain were forced from the valley, today's descendants once more gather in peaceful services in this beautiful church.

Founded by the Palatines, Stone Arabia, New York, takes its name from biblical Arabia Petrae (Arabia's capital of Petra). There are varied spellings and stories about how it got its name. One example is *Steen Rabi*, meaning "land of promise," which certainly fits the Palatines' reasons for coming to America. The name Stone Arabia was also given to settlements outside the valley. While near but not on Route 5, its connection cannot be denied. It was to Stone Arabia that many Palatines migrated. The two churches, locked in view of each other, are alive with that early history.

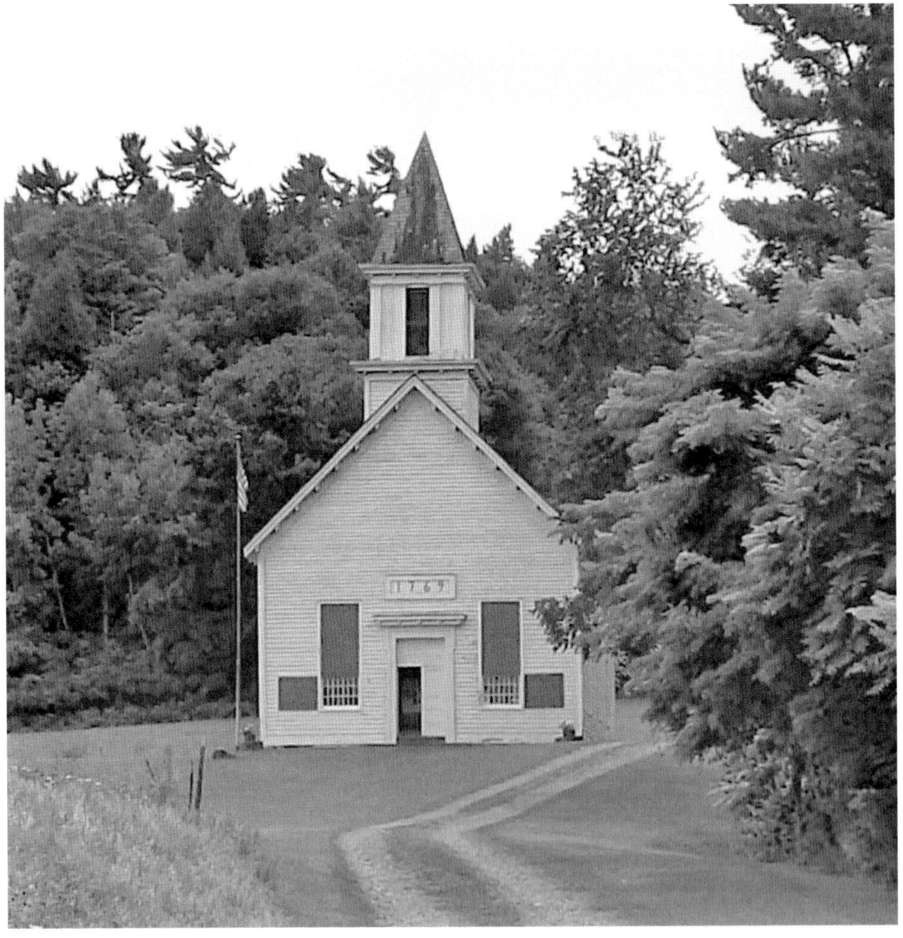

Indian Castle Church. *Courtesy of the author.*

Trinity Lutheran, built about 1729–32, was a log structure also constructed by the Palatines. Sir John Johnson's British forces burned it during the Battle of Stone Arabia in 1780. Rebuilt in 1792, it stands sentinel with its sister church over a cemetery that has pre-Revolutionary gravestones.

As with so much of the history during these early periods, we will find conflicting stories of how events unfolded. This is true of the rift between the Lutherans and Dutch Reformers over their log church. One story says the congregation argued over some now-forgotten incident; another claims the Lutheran and Reform doctrines were different enough that the two factions just split apart. Whichever is true, the two churches were built—the log church, or Trinity Lutheran, south of the existing lot and the exquisite limestone Reformed Dutch Church to the north.

The cemetery on the site of these churches is the resting place of Colonel John Brown from Pittsfield, Massachusetts, who organized the attack on Fort Ticonderoga in 1775. His forces were defeated at nearby Fort Paris.

Also having historic interest, if different in design from the Palatine churches, is Indian Castle Church, built in 1769 by Sir William Johnson. It sits on land donated by Joseph Brant and his sister Molly at the site of Upper Mohawk Castle. Built of clapboard, it is the last standing native missionary church of the colonial period. Indian Castle Church is located on Route 5S at Indian Castle, New York. With a graveyard behind it holding the remains of fallen white men and Indians alike, this small country church still houses events and services under a local preservation society. The tower bell survived a fire in 1979 and is original to the building.

ALSO OF THE VALLEY

The Mohawk Valley experienced many transformations following the Revolutionary War. These large changes also formed New York State. The Sullivan Campaign devastated the native way of life, while the military tract opened the frontier. Small settlements grew, new ones formed and native villages vanished into memory. From the Erie Canal's opening to discovery of natural mineral springs, wealth and industry entered the valley and moved westward. Religious fervor during the Second Great Awakening brought new ideas. The railroad and improved roads brought people in and carried them away. Some of what once was can still be seen; some must be imagined. The valley's contributions to the world are multiple, old and modern.

Nelliston

Nelliston, named for the Nellis family, is located on Route 5 near Fort Klock. The first to settle there was Andrew Nellis, who came in 1722.

Nellis Tavern, a home built in 1747 by Christian Nellis, faces Route 5, the King's Highway. The tavern was a popular meeting place and is a fine example of early American building and decoration. It is also very easy to see how much the road changed over the years. It would once have been at door level; now the building sits below the shoulder of

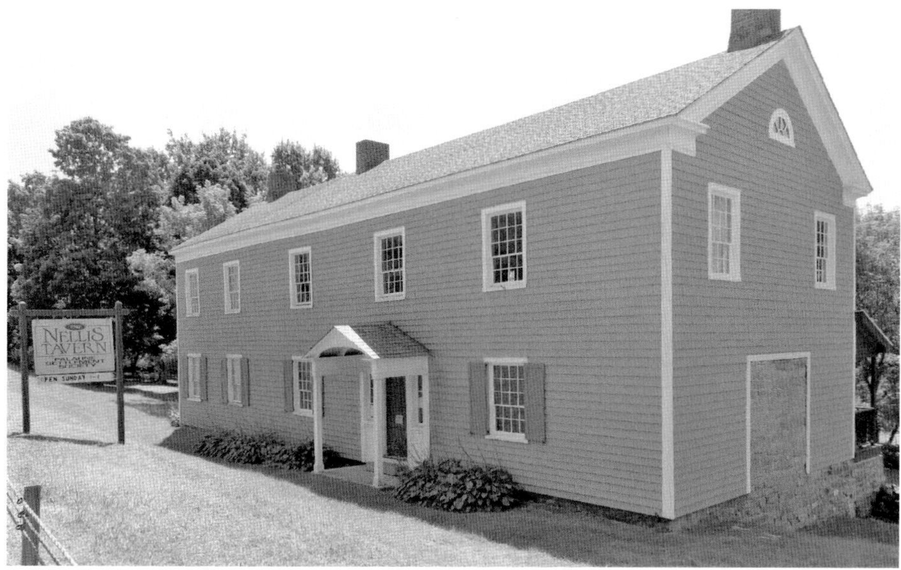

Nellis Tavern. *Courtesy of the author.*

the road. Open on Sundays, this landmark is under restoration by the Palatine Settlement Society.

Little Falls and Herkimer Home

Little Falls, just east of Herkimer, New York, on Route 5, is the site of General Nicholas Herkimer's home. In the 1800s, a significant stagecoach route ran from Rochester, passing through Little Falls on its way to Albany.

This location on the Mohawk River was an important native "carrying place" or portage. Once white colonies grew, they needed convenient ways to carry goods westward. Long before the Erie Canal was built, an earlier canal connected Little Falls with Lakes Oneida and Ontario via other small waterways. This Little Falls Canal was completed in 1795. It was New York State's first major canal. Its five wooden locks were later replaced with stone. Little Falls Canal was built north of the Mohawk River. Portions of it were later used to carry water via an aqueduct to the Erie Canal.

Although originally colonized by German Palatines, the mid- to late nineteenth century saw an influx of Roman Catholic Irish following the Great Potato Famine. The Irish were integral in building the Erie Canal.

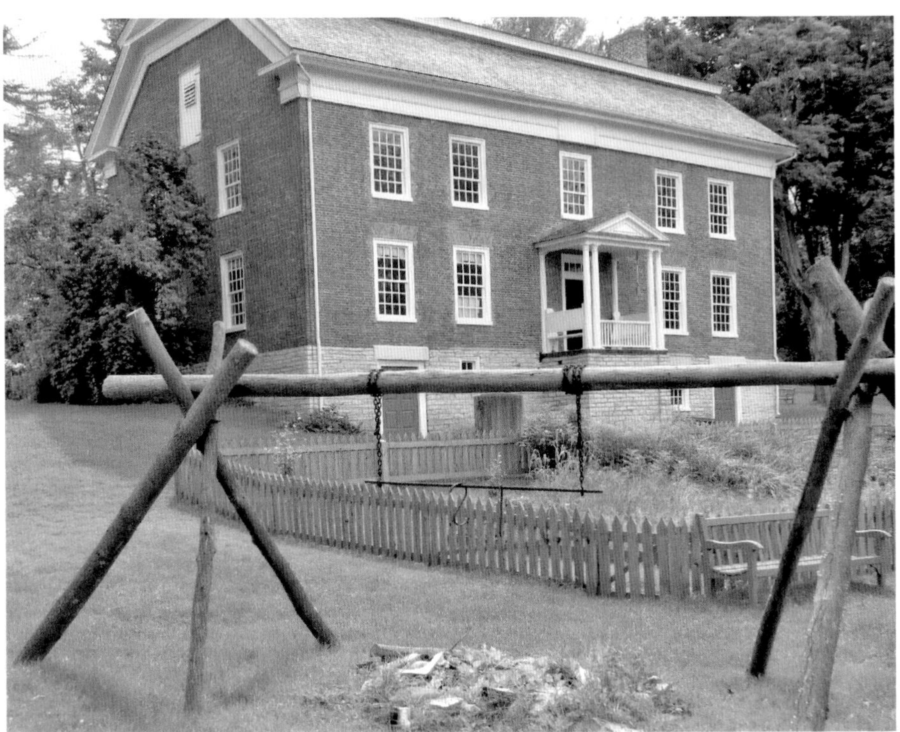

Herkimer Home. *Courtesy of the author.*

As a result of the canal and its accessibility, the woolens milled in Little Falls, as well as its cheeses and other manufactured goods, brought the tiny town statewide recognition during the highpoint of canal trade and travel.

Little Falls Canal is gone, and although the old Erie Canal was rerouted to carry larger barges, the new Erie Canal still travels through Little Falls. It is now merged with the Mohawk River. Boats must lock through due to the drop in elevation, and it is used mostly for recreation.

Man-made changes carved the landscape of Little Falls as surely as has nature. Moss Island is the result of removing rocks to make way for the Erie Canal, though prehistoric waterfalls made its many potholes. These waterfalls originated when the Great Lakes drained and glaciers blocked the St. Lawrence River. The cliffs of Moss Island are syenite and may be climbed if permits are obtained from the local police. Hikers will enjoy the trails. Moss Island is designated as a National Natural Landmark.

Natural riches and resources have always played a role in local economies. Not only will nature lovers find the region beautiful but

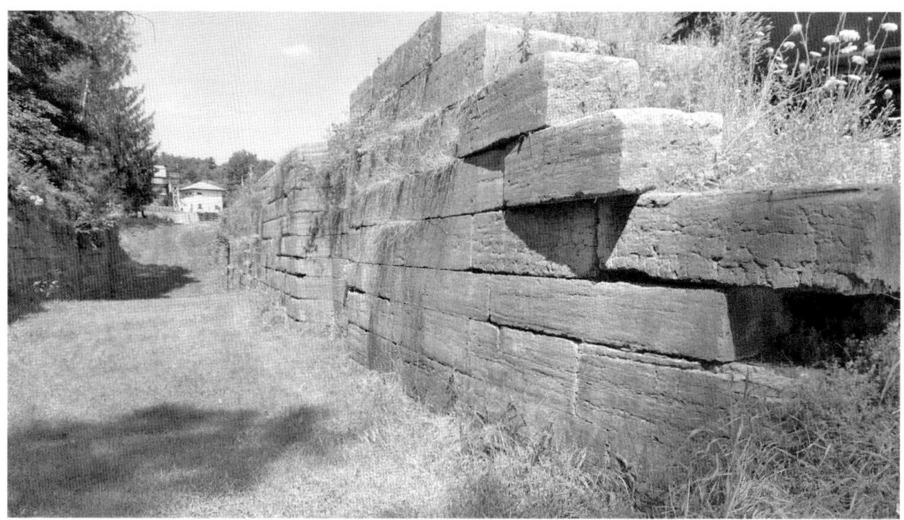

Old Erie Canal showing construction and narrow width. *Courtesy of the author.*

also adventurers can still partake in an old custom—that of mining for diamonds, of a sort.

New York State's crystals are valued for their clarity and at nearby Herkimer, travelers can pay a fee to dig at Herkimer Diamond Mine. This lustrous quartz dolostone, known today as Herkimer diamonds, was first discovered while digging near Little Falls and Middleville in the 18th century.

Ilion: Home of Remington Rifles

The village of Ilion is located in the town of Herkimer on Route 5S, south of the Mohawk River. As with many towns in New York State, Ilion's name is classical, for the ancient name of Troy.

Ilion has also undergone decades of transformation. It was at first Palatine. Very small, being no more than a store and a handful of homes, Ilion grew only when the Erie Canal was constructed. The canal built many towns, and when it no longer served a purpose, it also destroyed or changed those economies. However, Ilion had a saving grace: a company that helped it thrive. That company was the Remington Arms Company established by Eliphalet Remington in 1816, said to be the oldest company in the United States still making its original product. Quite a legacy!

Ilion had many names, including Steele's Creek, Morgan's Landing and New London. For a time, after Remington opened his company, the village was called Remington's Corners. It was eventually changed to Ilion on Remington's request.

The Remington Company diversified and, in 1856, began to also produce sewing machines, farm tools and typewriters. In this, we can see gradual societal changes in a settled country, no longer in fear of war or Indian attacks on a frontier. Steele's Creek, a nearby waterway, powered village factories. This was later harnessed so villagers could produce their own electricity.

The legendary Remington rifle is still manufactured in the "town Remington built." The story of how this rifle was born is a testimony to the industrial age and the inventor's passion.

Eliphalet Remington, named after his father, was born in a new nation in 1793 in Connecticut, a state that saw a revolution. The country was still a wild place, fresh off the War for Independence. It still required men to carry firearms to protect family, property and that fragile newfound freedom.

Eliphalet's young years also saw the birth of an industrial age. It is little wonder that Eliphalet's imagination was sparked, and he followed many other inventors who created as they found a need. His dream was to own a rifle better than those he could buy. He believed he could make such a gun and set out to prove it.

The Remington family settled near Utica, New York, in 1800. Eliphalet's father built a water-powered forge and smithy. No doubt, you've heard the expression: "He bought it lock, stock and barrel." If they were able, settlers bought all the parts at the same time. It was not uncommon, however, for poorer farmers to make their own rifles with purchased barrels. Eliphalet's father wanted to expand his business to make those barrels. So he sent his son on a buying trip to find sample barrels and observe techniques used for making them. Returning home, Eliphalet started his family on their way to production, after which he built the flintlock rifle of his dreams. Eliphalet took his masterpiece to a shooting match.

His new gun won second place in that match and so impressed the other competitors that, legend says, Eliphalet returned home with a "pocketful" of orders. Eliphalet Remington was now in the gun-making business. He moved his operation to Ilion in 1828, giving Ilion worldwide acclaim.

Utica: Beer and Insanity

Approximately thirty miles east of Oriskany Battlefield, along Route 5S, is the mid-sized city of Utica, seat of Oneida County. As a local tale says, when residents could not agree on a name for the town, they pulled suggestions from a hat. Yet another classical name was given to a valley settlement. Whether this is true or, as has been previously claimed, it was named by surveyor Robert Harpur, stories of how places were named remain part of our history's charm. Regardless, Utica is a typical example of how settlements begin with geography and people's needs.

This spot along the Mohawk River was one of the few shallows for fording the river. There are markers showing where General Herkimer's militia crossed and camped on their march toward today's Fort Stanwix. As a native crossroads, this location became a meeting place for traders and perfect for a settlement. Old Fort Schuyler, not to be confused with the later fort in Rome now called Fort Stanwix, was built at the crossroads of Utica in 1758. Permanently settled in 1773, Utica was one of many valley villages visited by George Washington on his later tour. A statue of him is found in front of the public library.

Although a bridge was built over the Mohawk at this point in 1792, it was demolished during a spring flood very shortly after so that Utica did not grow significantly until the Great Genesee Road was created in 1794. With an excellent road and little fear of attack, travelers and stagecoaches flowed freely on their way to and from Albany. This made it necessary to have horses cared for, as well as places to rest while waiting for mounts to be tended. As a result, blacksmith Moses Bagg became quite the entrepreneur, opening a shabby tavern to meet this need. His small "watering-hole" on Main Street eventually grew into a fine two-story inn and tavern known as Bagg's Hotel. It remained in the Bagg family for years, hosting many well-known visitors, including Thomas Moore, Joseph Bonaparte, Aaron Burr and Washington Irving. Bagg's Hotel became the Northern Hotel, catching fire in 1870. Moses Bagg Jr. later built Shepard's Hotel across from the site of the Northern. Today, a park is located in the city district known as Bagg's Square, once the site of Bagg's Hotel.

Utica's population in 1817 was just under three thousand people, making it a fair size by comparison to other villages between it and Albany. It was self-sufficient by that time, with its own newspaper, bank, five churches and many businesses. The city experienced another boom with the Erie Canal. Utica is considered one of the most rapidly growing cities of the nineteenth and twentieth centuries.

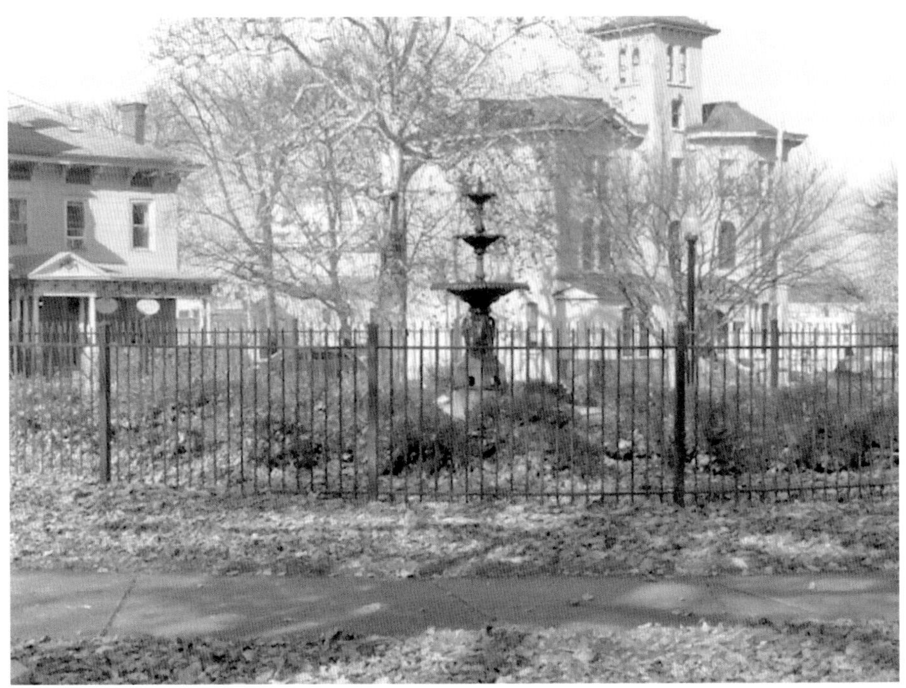

Rutger-Steuben Park, once-stately homes and a central park represent the golden age of industry and wealth. *Courtesy of photographer and graphic designer Charles Burke.*

The city's story is tied to the railroads—and, later, roadways—that changed the course of travel to Utica and therefore the population and economy. One needs only to visit Utica's Rutger-Steuben Park to see the architecture of the city's high period of opulence.

Utica's history is also one of pop culture. Perhaps its most famous native is none other than one of Disney's favorite Mouseketeers: Annette Funicello, born there in October 1942. However, Annette's family moved to California four years later, leaving her story seldom connected with Utica.

Many people of the 1950s generation may also recall two well-known spokesmen for Utica Club beer: Schultz and Dooley animated-character beer steins. These two characters represented the West End Brewing Company of Utica. Puppeteer Bill Baird breathed life into the mugs, while famed comedian Jonathan Winters created their German and Irish voices.

The West End Brewing Company began during the city's industrial period, circa 1888. Prior to that time, the location had housed Charles Bierbauer

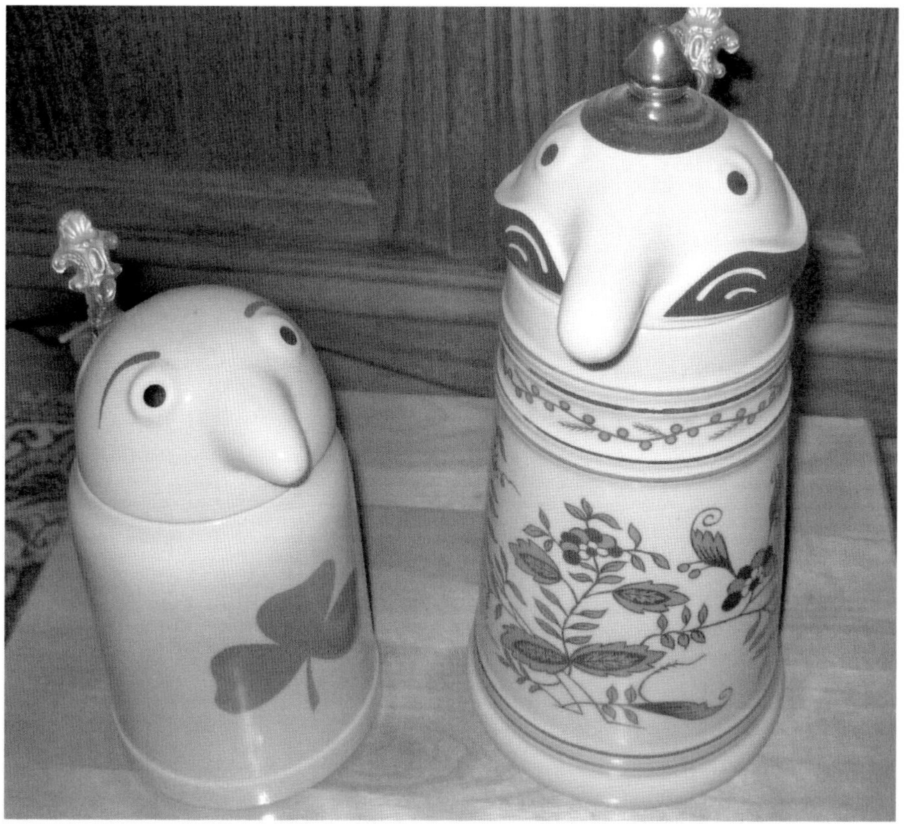

Shultz and Dooley beer steins, Utica Club beer. *Courtesy of Joan Oblinsky Scharf.*

Brewery. During Prohibition, West End survived by making nonalcoholic beverages under the moniker Utica Club so as not to confuse its customers. Utica Club continued as the brand name even after Prohibition was lifted. There is little doubt for many that Utica is the playful city beer built, but it has a darker history, too, as one of many cities that housed the insane.

New York State Lunatic Asylum

When a country becomes peaceful, it can turn its thoughts to that of creating beauty, and its population grows. However, with population also comes the need to care for those who cannot care for themselves. History is replete with stories of the poor and insane often given identical treatment. It was commonplace to simply throw these people into "prisons" established for the safety of society, more so than for the welfare of the inmate. This is as true of America as it was of Europe in those days. Debtors' prisons overflowed with invalids and indigents.

Our collective literary memory is also filled with strange stories of the crazy uncle or invalid child nobody could control kept in secret rooms of an old mansion. While spooky, these were the fortunate few. The poor did not often have the benefit of family care. They ended up in prison, begging on streets or dead.

Enos Throop, in his duties as governor of New York State, signed legislation ending imprisonment of debtors in 1831. He supported establishing asylums for the insane poor—those whose families could not afford appropriate care. Even though methods used in those early institutions haunt us, for their time, they were the best the system could offer.

By the late 1800s, most institutions for the mentally disabled were using the "moral treatment." Dr. Thomas Story Kirkbridge created a philosophy for both the architecture and care of mental patients under this treatment. However, he was not first to use this concept. Kirkbridge might have been influenced by the first director of the New York State Lunatic Asylum, Dr. Amariah Brigham, one of the founders of the American Psychiatric Association. Brigham believed the best treatment for patients included their

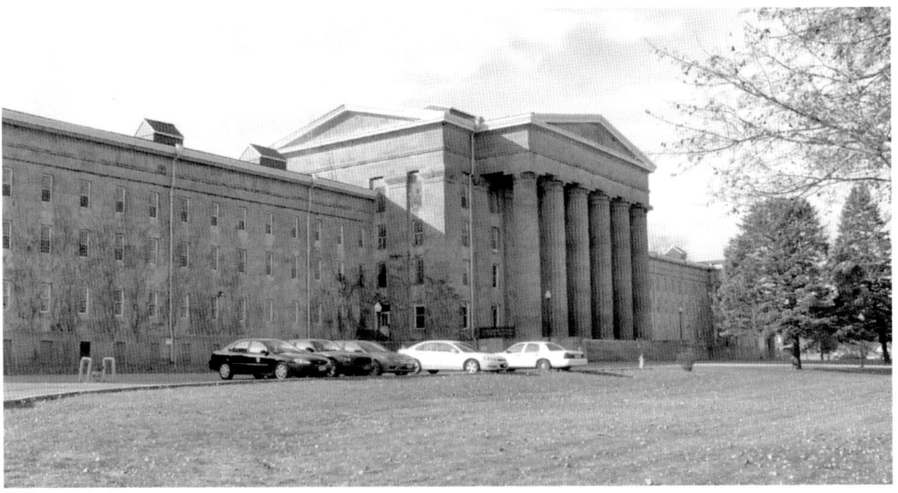

Utica Lunatic Asylum, now housing Department of Mental Health New York State records. *Courtesy of photographer and graphic designer Charles Burke.*

occupation in these facilities. Part of his work as director was to set up a print shop at the asylum, and it was there that he created the first *American Journal of Insanity*, today's *American Journal of Psychiatry*. Even the inmates were allowed to print their own journal, the *Opal*.

New York State Lunatic Asylum, later named Utica Psychiatric Center or Utica State Hospital, was the first asylum in the state, as well as one of the first in the country. The structure, designed by Captain William Clarke and funded with state and private money, was originally intended to have four buildings with connecting verandas that met to form a thirteen-acre octagonal space. Funding constraints made it possible for only one structure to be initially built. The asylum, which opened to patients in 1843, included a farm of over one hundred acres where food for the inmates was raised. Additional produce sold helped pay the institution's expenses. Approximately 276 patients were admitted within that first year. Filling quickly, wings were added to the building, opening to additional patients by 1846. Partially destroyed by fire in 1852, the asylum, known to locals as "Old Main," continued in service until 1978, when patients were transferred elsewhere. Today, a portion of the building is used to store records for New York State's Department of Mental Health.

Dr. Brigham died in 1849. However, the benefits of Dr. Brigham's work were felt long after his passing. Barbaric by today's standards, he set into motion ideas that changed how we view our mentally challenged friends and

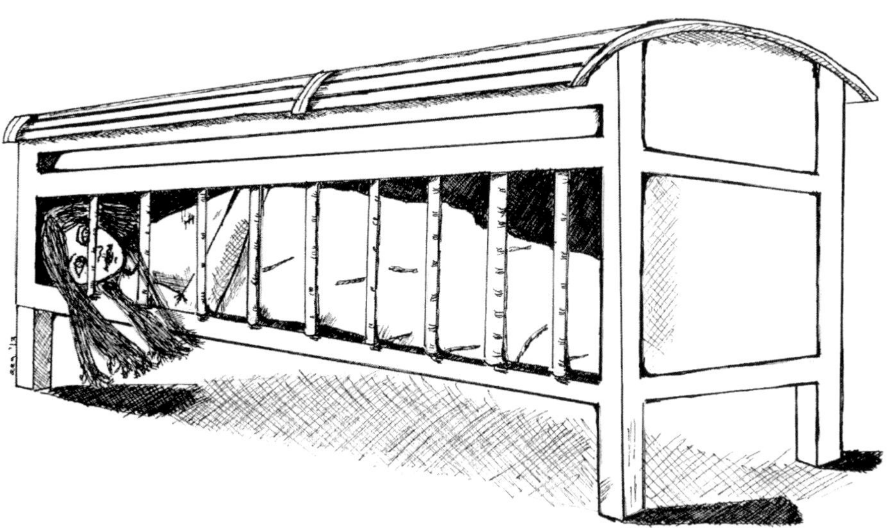

The Utica Crib, used to treat mental patients. *Courtesy of artist Alice Gerard.*

family. Although bizarre, one of his greatest contributions was the infamous Utica Crib.

Based on a French design, this adult-sized apparatus was completely enclosed by spindles just like a baby's crib with a top to secure the patient. The spindles allowed for airflow. An early design even allowed the crib to be suspended for gentle rocking to calm the inhabitant.

Brigham believed this treatment had a comforting, protective effect, the perfect match to his philosophy that treatment of the insane should consist of rest, quiet, seclusion and dietary monitoring. His treatment design included no chains or darkened pits, like at many other hospitals of the time. Still, using the Utica Crib was controversial. Although some patients reported liking it over other treatments that restrained their arms and legs, proponents of the moral movement, such as Dr. Tuke from Europe, felt the crib was more like a cage for animals. Regardless, Utica Cribs remained in use at the hospital until 1887 and were utilized at many other facilities around the country. One is housed in a collection at the Western Illinois Museum.

Vernon: Oneida Castle

As pioneers moved across the state, they encountered various natives already inhabiting the lands—or at least, remnants of them. The Oneidas, friendly to the Americans, were one of two tribes given reservations, ironically on lands once their territory. Vernon was a major Oneida village.

Quite a few smaller towns along Route 5 were established because of waterways that allowed industries to flourish. Vernon, New York, is one of these communities. Sconondoa Creek with its drop in elevation made it possible for the settlement to grow in unison with several sawmills, gristmills, tanneries, a carding mill and a distillery. Nearby trees also gave rise to three glass factories that used the wood to heat glass ovens. However, these glass factories were forced to relocate when fuel resources ran out. Even with its many industries over the years, farming, especially dairy farming, remained Vernon's main source of income.

The small village's population grew after the Great Genesee Road was built. Vernon, once the site of several early educational facilities, is currently best known to have the state's fastest harness racing track. Turning Stone, a native casino, operates nearby.

Skenandoah Boulder

The Oneidas are the "People of the Standing Stone," which is the meaning of their name, *Onyota'ake*. Legend says a great stone led the people and where it stopped, they settled. Other versions exist, one stating that an enemy who chased the Oneida could not find them because the Oneida turned to stone and another that a great stone appeared in their villages to give them direction. Possibly this was a metaphor for their sachems, one such as Skenandoah.

Oskanondonha "the Deer," or commonly known as Skenandoah, was an Oneida war chief. He led the Oneidas against the French in the French and Indian War. His legend is one of friendship to the settlers. By scouting the Mohawk Valley during the Revolutionary War, Skenandoah supported the Americans against the British. His warnings, including one given to the people of German Flatts, saved many settlers' lives. Skenandoah's warriors fought with General Herkimer at Oriskany, and it was Skenandoah's people who brought corn to George Washington's troops at Valley Forge.

Chief Skenandoah's mission to Albany in 1775 is a very sad account of a great man's betrayal. Several of his so-called friends got him drunk on alcohol. He was found the next morning, facedown in a street gutter, stripped of all his belongings, including his clothes and regalia. This, according to legend, is why he never drank alcohol again and urged his people to have none:[*] "Drink no firewater of the white man. It makes you mice for the white men who are cats. Many a meal they have eaten of you."

Skenandoah's aged years brought him blindness. He is said to have lived over one hundred years, until he died at Oneida Castle on March 11, 1816. Skenandoah is buried in Hamilton, New York, next to his missionary friend Samuel Kirkland. Skenandoah's Boulder marks the spot of his one-time home and is located just outside the town limits of Oneida Castle on Route 5. A New York State historical sign is also posted there.

> *I am an aged hemlock. The winds of a hundred winters have whistled through my branches. I am dead at the top. The generation to which I have belonged has run away and left me. Why I live the Great Spirit only knows.*
> *—an aging Skenandoah to his people.*

*. As with the other stories in this book, several sources were compared to create this story. One source is the Native Heritage Project at http://nativeheritageproject.com/2012/05/29/oneida-chief-skenandoah.

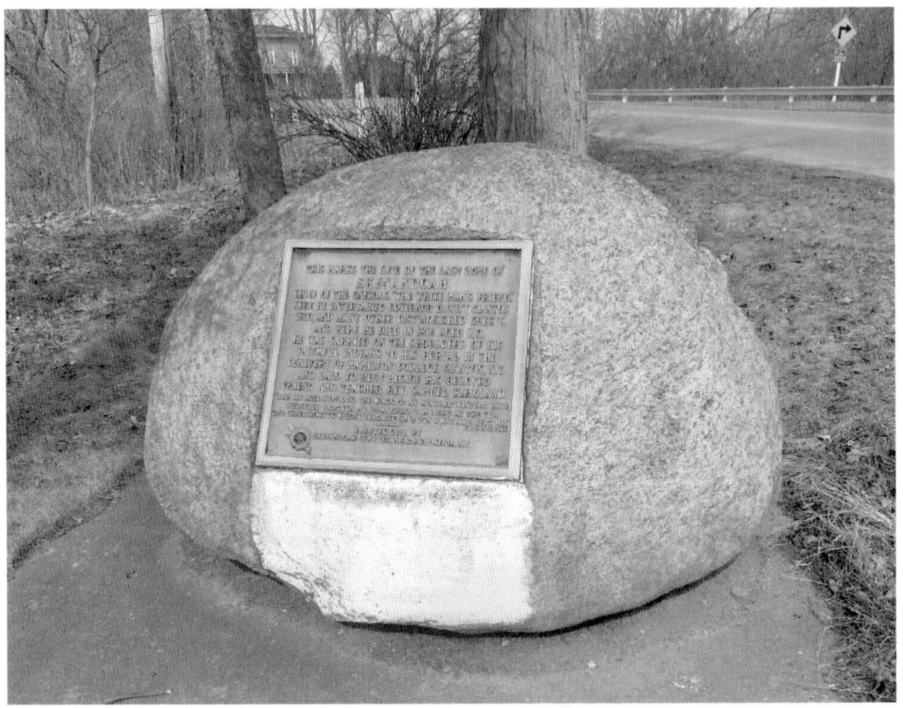

Skenandoah's Boulder and marker showing the location of Chief Skenandoah's lodge. *Courtesy of storyteller Susanna Connelly Holstein.*

We owe much to this great leader and his people. Their support of white settlers cost the Oneidas their land, homes and way of life. Even after the newly formed Congress applauded the Oneidas for their service, they were forced out by an increasing number of pioneers. Many went to Canada and some to Wisconsin when native peoples were driven westward. All that remains of the six million acres that once belonged to the Oneidas is a thirty-two-acre reservation in Madison County. As the legends say, the Great Standing Stone that guided the Oneida will appear again only when they are reunited.

City of Oneida

The region of Oneida in Madison County on Route 5 was a reservation set aside for the tribe following the Revolution until the early 1800s. Gradual migration of businesses, incorporation of the road and the Erie Canal brought more and more white settlers until they eventually supplanted the Oneidas as the majority.

Sands Higinbotham was responsible for Oneida's financial growth. Higinbotham owned and operated Oneida Depot. When the New York Central Railroad needed right of way through his property, this sly businessman struck the deal—the railroad promised that his depot would be a regular stop. Soon, people, commerce and money followed. As with Moses Bagg of Utica, Higinbotham grasped the opportunity this afforded him, building both a hotel and a restaurant at his station. This made Oneida Depot one of the state's earliest roadside rest stops. It was due to Higinbotham's entrepreneurial spirit that a variety of goods were produced, from furniture to carriages to caskets. With the canal and these goods, Oneida became a serious player in trade. Even so, Oneida is best known for Oneida Limited, the world's largest maker of stainless steel and silver-plated flatware. What many might not know is that this Oneida company had its beginning in the utopian movement that built several communities along Routes 5 and 20, one of which was Oneida Community.

Bouckville's Landmark Tavern

Bouckville, named for canal commissioner William C. Bouck, is located at the crossroads of the Cherry Valley Turnpike and Chenango Canal, just five miles east of Morrisville. This hamlet remained quite small until the Chenango Canal was built. Its industries included cider making and a distillery. It was in Bouckville that Samuel R. Mott made apple cider and vinegar, becoming a lasting legacy when he founded Motts Company in 1847. Two taverns operated in the early days, McClure Tavern and Crain House. Neither is in operation today. However, there is one that was not built to be a tavern.

Contradictory information surrounds current-day Landmark Tavern. Some attribute James Cooledge (Coolidge) of hops fame as its builder. This Cooledge raised the first hops grown in Madison County and was first to mass-produce hops in the country. The tavern's builder might in fact have been his son by the same name.

Bouckville's Landmark Tavern is unique in its design and history. Built about 1851, construction presented a problem. Cooledge originally planned his building to be octagonal, with twenty-four-foot walls per side. The lot

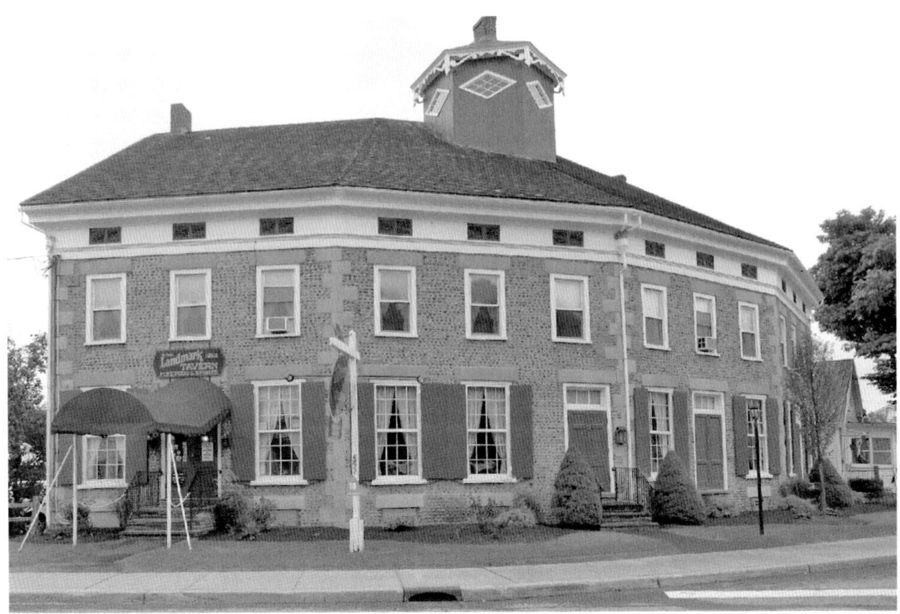

Landmark Tavern, Bouckville. *Courtesy of the author.*

wasn't large enough, so he solved this conundrum with four sides facing the roads and two other sides forming a wedge at the back. A cupola was placed on top, in keeping with the style of the day. Legend has it that the cupola has six sides, one for each of his previous five wives and one for a woman who died before they could be married, though new knowledge disputes the story.

His intention was not to build a tavern but rather what we might call the first "shopping mall." The building had several merchants inside, including a dressmaker, a hardware store, a grocery and an emporium. Its location made a very convenient stop for travelers and stagecoaches.

Today, the Landmark Tavern is a restaurant with several second-story rooms to rent by the night.

Morrisville, Town that Crime and Farming Built

Settled by Thomas Morris in 1776 and originally named Morris Flats, this small hamlet grew into a larger town as the seat of Madison County from 1817 to 1907. Its history is connected with the Mohawk Valley's most important economy: agriculture. In 1908, Morrisville was home to the New York State School of Agriculture. It is always interesting to find what helped such small settlements grow and continue to exist without huge conglomerates at their center. Today, the school is part of the New York State University system still offering many programs in various areas of farming.

Early travel was possible on Route 20, if slow and unreliable. Therefore, those associated with county government resided nearby, including judges and lawyers. Jurors and witnesses needed accommodations when trials were underway. Hotels, boardinghouses and businesses to serve the populace followed. However, there were other industries.

In the mid-1800s, cast-iron stoves overtook fireplaces for home heating. A foundry opened in Morrisville in 1830 for production of those stoves. In that industrial age, many other factories opened, making everything from combs and furniture to beer. Interestingly, the United States once had a very small silk industry, and there was a silk mill in Morrisville. The largest of local industries was the tannery, although it closed when regional hemlock bark was exhausted.

All of these industries aside, it was the county seat that sustained the village. Of course, Morrisville's very own gang of outlaws kept the court busy.

The Loomis Gang

Located in traditional Oneida territory, Waterville, "Hops Capital of the World," was first settled following the American Revolution after the Oneidas were forced to give up their lands. Called "The Huddle" until the name became Waterville in 1808, and located about one mile north of Route 20 on Route 12, the village was the birthplace of George Eastman, founder of the Eastman Kodak Company. Sangerfield, named after Jedediah Sanger, lies south of Waterville en route to Route 20. Both towns fostered many industries similar to others in the region, with Waterville producing hops that were shipped worldwide, but there is a seedier history. This was the stomping ground for the infamous Loomis Gang, a family of outlaws and horse thieves.

Route 20 touches Nine Mile Swamp's northern tip, once known by the Oneidas as Great Swamp. A road running through the swamp is named for the Loomises. The swamp abounds with tales of ghosts, many connected with the gang. A nearby hill called Loomis Hill served as a lookout point for the gang, which used its marshy landscape to hide its loot.

The matriarchal Loomis Gang was the nation's largest robber gang in the nineteenth century, at one time touting over two hundred members. Its story begins with George Washington Loomis and his young, wild bride, Rhoda Mallet (Mallette), who largely controlled their activities.

Keeping in mind that many of these older stories were passed by word of mouth and became legend, we can only attempt to piece together some fact blended with fiction. As with most of these tales, we find variances. One such rendition says George Loomis's father came to America from England in the colonial period, becoming highly respected in Connecticut society. George grew up in Connecticut and was later chased across state borders by a posse after he stole a horse. In 1802, he sought refuge with his sister Clarissa in Sangerfield, New York, where he eventually met Rhoda Mallet, the well-educated, young, beautiful and "tempestuous" daughter of an officer of the French Revolution who was convicted of embezzlement. Perhaps there is something to be said for the apple not falling far from the tree? Rhoda married George, and together they raised ten children.

George and Rhoda reared their offspring with their own special brand of parenting, which included Rhoda reportedly telling them, "You may steal, but if you are caught, you shall be whipped." One might wonder if this was a stern threat against stealing, except that other tales say she fed them and sent the children off to steal whatever they could, "even if it is nothing but a jackknife." George was apparently no better, teaching his children to steal, bribe, threaten and counterfeit.

The couple's second son, George Washington Loomis Jr., known commonly as "Wash," became the gang's best asset. He was a smooth sweet-talker with an easy style. Rhoda arranged for Wash to study in a law office—a clever way, she felt, of teaching him inside information that would help the gang later. Their third son, Grove, had his father's propensity for "walking off" with somebody else's horse. Eventually, others outside the family joined the Loomis Gang, giving it widespread reach.

The litany of accusations against them ranged from horse thievery, a very serious frontier offense, to burglary, robbery and counterfeiting. Some say they were even likely to take another man's laundry right off the clothesline.

The gang made sure to treat locals fairly because they knew their neighbors would help hide them. They also bribed local law enforcement, and "mysterious" fires started in buildings belonging to anyone who opposed the gang, with the accused arsonist always having an alibi. They hired the best lawyers when they needed them.

Even so, in 1848, angry neighbors raided the Loomis homestead, finding evidence of their thievery there and throughout the swamp. In 1849, Wash decided it was time to "get out of Dodge." He followed speculators heading west to seek gold in California, returning a year later, in 1850. Activity had slowed in Wash's absence, but despite his father's death one year after he returned, the gang managed to stay on top of its game for another decade, spreading a network of mayhem from Canada south to the Pennsylvania border and east to Vermont.

Several members of the gang were arrested for horse thievery, perhaps after attempting to sell stolen horses to the Union army during the Civil War. Their trial was set to be held at the Madison County Courthouse in Morrisville, but not so inexplicably, on October 10, 1864, it burned to the ground, along with evidence against the gang. Still, court convened next day at Exchange Hotel across the street, but evidence was insufficient at that point. It was nearly one year later, on October 30, 1865, when a vigilante group attacked the Loomises' farm, killing Wash Loomis. Then, in 1866, someone finally burned the place. Rhoda fled with two children to Hastings, New York.

The Loomis Gang's reign was over, but its legend continues in our imaginations. Now drained, much of Nine Mile Swamp is farmland, though some people say Wash Loomis's ghost still roams there.

Chittenango and The Wizard of Oz

Chittenango is an Oneida word meaning "where the sun shines out." This village is a quintessential canal town, built to serve the Erie Canal, which officially opened just to the north in 1825. A smaller canal was built to connect the village with the Erie Canal, bringing goods and people. Chittenango Boat Landing also served the Erie Canal with three dry-dock bays for repairing and building boats. All the amenities required by travelers grew in the village—hotels, inns, restaurants, factories, farms, mills, shops, banks, a fire company, a newspaper and churches. However, Chittenango's greatest claim to fame, and current draw, is its annual *Wizard of Oz* festival: "Oz-Stravaganza." Many small towns have festivals to help their economy, such as "best scarecrow" contests where residents display their handmade scarecrows for prizes. They didn't invent the scarecrow, but Chittenango *did* invent *The Wizard of Oz* by giving birth to the author.

Lyman Frank Baum was born in Chittenango in 1856. A prolific writer, Baum not only wrote *The Wonderful Wizard of Oz*, which became a 1939 Hollywood sensation, but he also penned fifty-five novels, over two hundred poems, eighty-three short stories and a plethora of other manuscripts. Some say he envisioned several technological advancements from televisions to laptop computers. Perhaps this beloved author's only societal flaw was his philosophy relating to Native Americans. He believed they should be eradicated. However, Baum was in support of the women's movement. Lyman Baum, native to Chittenango, was more commonly called by his middle name, Frank. He died in Hollywood at age sixty-two and is buried in Forest Lawn in Glendale, California.

Pompey

A very small rural community, Pompey was part of the Military Tract divvied out to soldiers of the Revolutionary War. Some growth took place when the Erie Canal opened, and many Irish workers on the canal settled there, establishing a sound agricultural economy. Pompey is also home to a legendary grindstone used by the Onondaga Indians to sharpen their weapons. Commonly referred to as the Indian War Stone, it now resides at Lemoyne Park.

Another wonder from Pompey is the Cardiff Giant of nearby Cardiff, New York. Now located at the Farmers' Museum in Cooperstown, the Cardiff Giant was one of the largest hoaxes perpetrated on American soil.

In 1869, thousands of thrill-seeking tourists flocked to see this ten-foot stone giant dug up by workmen in a farmer's field. They paid a whopping fifty cents to view the spectacle. Everyone had a theory, and debates abounded. The giant might have been a long-lost antiquity or, as followers of the Perfectionist movement thought, one of the giants that live in the earth as mentioned in the Bible. Some even believed a Jesuit missionary carved the statue. There was no shortage of curiosity over this strange being. In fact, with some really good publicity, the stone giant sold to businessmen from Syracuse for over $37,000.

During an era of the traveling exhibition, when Americans thirsted for knowledge, even intellects from the country's finest universities pondered its origins. P.T. Barnum himself tried to buy the giant, but when the owners refused, he had a copy made from plaster. It was on display in New York

City and drew even bigger audiences than the original. The owners tried to sue Barnum, but since they could not prove that their own stone being was genuine, the suit was dropped.

The truth? Well, it is not as romantic as all that. Tobacconist George Hull had argued with a local Methodist minister about whether the Bible should be taken word for word. The minister was a Perfectionist; Hull, an atheist. He paid a sculptor to chisel the statue and buried it in the field of his friend William Newell, where he knew Newell wanted workers to dig a well. Finally debunked by Yale paleontologist Othniel C. Marsh, Hull had to confess to the hoax. The truly amazing thing is that not only did people continue to travel to see it but it also still attracted Barnum and his audiences.

Cardiff, New York, is just off Route 20, west of Pompey.

The Swampland that Became Syracuse

Several other names graced Syracuse before it was finalized in 1820, at the start of America's Industrial Revolution. Its eventual name comes from Siracusa, a village in Sicily. Formally laid out in 1819, Syracuse is the state's fifth-largest city and the western bookend of the Mohawk Valley. The village became a city in the mid-nineteenth century, when it merged with Salina, named for the salt found there. Bypassed completely by Route 20 and the New York State Thruway, Syracuse anchors Route 5 to Albany and Buffalo. Syracuse, with its central location, is home to the New York State Fair.

Someone once said, "Location, location, location." Nothing could be more true when it comes to building a city. Syracuse, once a salty, barren swampland, has been the state crossroads for both the Erie Canal and the railroad. Today, it is the crossroads of Thruway 90 and Interstate 81.

Syracuse is sometimes referred to as the Salt City because the region once lay beneath an ancient salt sea. That sea left behind beds of salt and limestone, two natural resources that encouraged economic growth.

The city's settlement was largely due to Onondaga Lake, named for the Onondaga members of the Iroquois Confederacy who called the region home for thousands of years. The Onondagas' first European contact was with the French when Samuel de Champlain attacked them in 1615. About forty years later, the Onondagas were exposed to Christianity. Legends say a Jesuit missionary, Father Simon LeMoyne, drank from a nearby spring that local natives believed poisoned by evil spirits. Knowing instantly that it was salt, the priest took a sampling back to Canada. A mission was built near the salt bed in 1656, changing the Onondagas' lives forever.

In 1751, with the French befriending the natives and setting up strongholds, British Indian agent Sir William Johnson countered with an offer to buy the lands within miles around Lake Onondaga. This agreement made those lands a British conquest, later falling into American hands.

As elsewhere, the British and Americans gradually usurped Indian territories. Since the Onondagas had sided with England during the Revolutionary War, they were stripped of their lands, which were then sold off to salt companies. However, the Onondagas were among the "enemy" tribes that accepted an offer of reservation lands, along with the Senecas and Cayugas. The other tribes left for Canada. Over the following years, the Onondagas slowly sold off their land in exchange for trade goods. This trade with the local native population had an economic bolstering effect as more settlers gravitated to the area for that purpose. In the end, however, the Onondagas ended up with nothing except hunting and fishing rights.

Much of what is now Syracuse was either a salt reservoir or a gloomy swamp, where disease killed many salt boilers before the mire was drained and settled. On a positive note, the area's westernmost portion was well forested with valuable timber—hemlock for tanning and cedar, birch, maple and pine for building. However, salt remained its most valuable asset. Even nearby Fairmount, home to engineer, surveyor and politician James Geddes, was part of the salt reserve.

When the War of 1812 made it difficult for Americans to import salt, Syracuse's salt industry experienced an upsurge. Later, the Erie Canal, which ran right through the village, increased the sale of salt again. Most of this salt was used to preserve products being transported on the canal to keep them from spoiling.

Salt built Syracuse, and Syracuse was as salty as the canawlers who passed through on the canal. Establishments making up Syracuse's canal front were hotels, taverns, shops and factories. There might also have been stables for tow mules, as well as blacksmiths and harness makers. The canal created economy in every place it touched, and Syracuse was no exception.

Syracuse was also on the road to freedom. Slaves escaping during the Civil War to Canada, and points east in New England, found the Underground Railroad alive in Syracuse. The city remains famous as one of the railroad's most significant stops.

After the Civil War, when the salt industry waned, the Industrial Revolution took over. Factories produced a wide array of merchandise, from soda ash, which utilized the salt and limestone resources, to traffic lights and the Franklin Car, produced by Franklin Automobile Company. Industry ensured that when the canal and railroads no longer proved useful, and New York State's Thruway rerouted traffic, the city of Syracuse would survive. Its population grew exponentially up through World War II, when it declined steadily in favor of suburban life.

Camillus: One Sharp Town

Fifteen minutes west of Syracuse is Camillus, home to one of the country's oldest knife companies, Camillus Cutlery. Originating in 1876, it sent quality knives worldwide. Founded by a German named Adolph Kastor, this company employed and housed many German craftsmen. Over time, it manufactured not only knives for hunting but also surgical scalpels, a folding knife/spoon set for the Red Cross, folding knives for the Boy Scouts of America and many knives sent to allies during World War II. Its products have held the private labels of Woolworth, Sears and Craftsman. Although it went bankrupt in 2006, Acme United acquired the company and still produces signature pieces by Les Stroud "Survivorman."

Elbridge: Home of a Legend

In the green and silent valley.
"There he sang of Hiawatha,
Sang the Song of Hiawatha,
Sang his wondrous birth and being,
How he prayed and how be fasted,
How he lived, and toiled, and suffered,
That the tribes of men might prosper,
That he might advance his people!"
—Henry Wadsworth Longfellow

Captain William Stevens, whose family was second to settle this piece of Military Tract, named the village for Elbridge Gerry, a signer of the

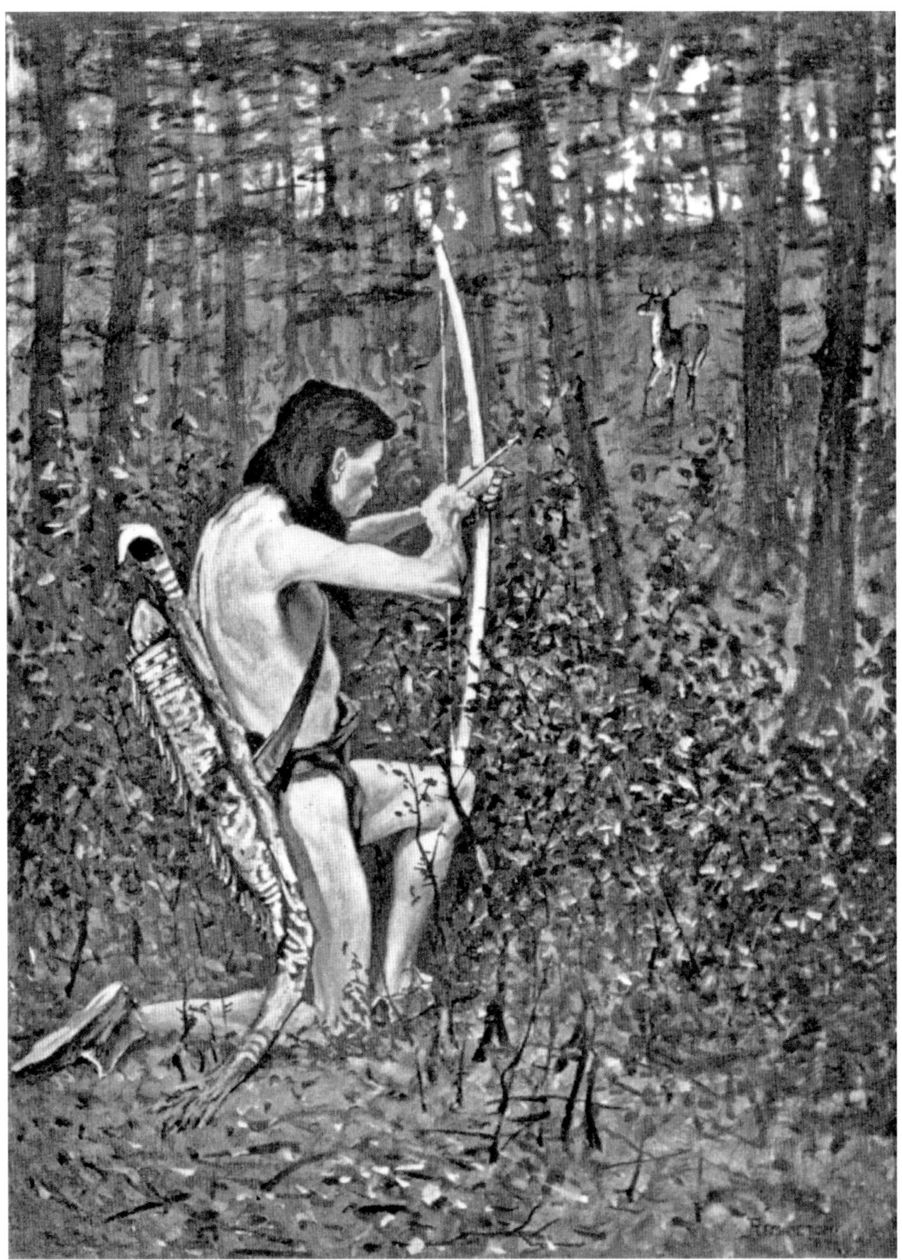

"[T]hen upon one knee, uprising, Hiawatha aimed an arrow." *Courtesy of the Library of Congress, Prints and Photographs Division.*

Declaration of Independence. Gerry was once governor of Massachusetts and fifth vice president of the United States. Both men participated in the Boston Tea Party.

Natural resources and pioneer needs spurred village growth. Its story is much like that of other towns in the region, but there is a story that sets Elbridge aside from the others.

A fortified Native American village rested on the banks of Cross Lake, a widening in the Seneca River touching the northern end of Jordan. It is rumored to have been home to Chief Hiawatha, the legendary and historical co-founder of the Iroquois Confederacy.

Facts about Hiawatha's life are conflicting. He lived sometime between the eleventh and sixteenth centuries. Hiawatha was chief of the Onondagas or Mohawks—or possibly both. We know little of his origins, other than he might have been Onondaga and later adopted by the Mohawks. Hiawatha's prowess as an orator helped convince the tribes to follow the "Great Peacemaker" Dekanawida's vision of unity. Chief Hiawatha was entrusted with the wampum of the Great Law, as well as treaties, and the right to announce decisions made by the Grand Council of Chiefs. The famous poem by Henry Wadsworth Longfellow does not tell Hiawatha's story; rather, it tells of Nanabozho, an Ojibwa. Nonetheless, Hiawatha's name lives in the hearts of all who have heard the poem. He was a great leader.

HEALING WATERS

Early European settlers flocked to the New World for many reasons, most desiring freedom of one kind or another. Of course, we are reminded that there were others here before. Native peoples knew the resources we can only pretend to have discovered. Many settlements became spas around natural sulfur springs, revered by native peoples. Later, white settlers utilized them for healing and bolstering their economy.

The spa period ran from approximately 1800 to 1860. In some cases, these resorts remained open into the early 1900s. One of the earliest spas was Richfield Springs, known by the Indians as "Big Mineral Waters."

Richfield Springs

This Route 20 village of fewer than two thousand residents has many beautiful homes, refurbished within the past two decades. Originally a split from Otsego in 1792, the village is named for nearby springs. These sulfur springs have long attracted people for their curative properties over various skin ailments. Its fabulous homes are a testament to the 1800s and early 1900s, when Richfield Springs was a premier resort, bringing the wealthy from many larger cities. East Main Street is on the National Register of Historic Places with dozens of private residences, boardinghouses, a theater, a post office, a church and a one-time hotel, most dating from 1836 to 1942.

The resort movement in Richfield Springs began with Dr. Horace Manley. He bought Great White Sulphur Springs, the "purest mineral water in the world," and built a bathhouse. Manley had twenty-five patients to begin his venture. That was the start of something big, as they say. As more and more people came for the baths and hotels, other commercial and residential properties grew, too. At the spa season's height, some local hotels held from one hundred to five hundred people, rivaling many of today's lodgings. Hotels, now gone, included the American, International, Berkeley and Kendallwood. One might still see the lower two levels of the International.

A park now marks the location of Springs Hotel that burned in 1897. Many of the park's trees might predate the old hotel. Most of the other resort hotels were torn down to make way for more useful commercial buildings following the resort era's end. Springs Hotel was not rebuilt as waning tourism dictated. A nineteenth-century waterworks with fountains, a pumping house and landscaping is included in the state registry. A lovely bandstand and four-sided clock were added to the park in the early 1900s.

During the spa's high period, the Lackawanna Railroad stopped here, carrying many visitors year round. The trains later carried only freight. Railroad service continued for 150 years through about 1920, until automobiles became the major mode of travel. The Great Depression played a significant role in Richfield Springs' decline.

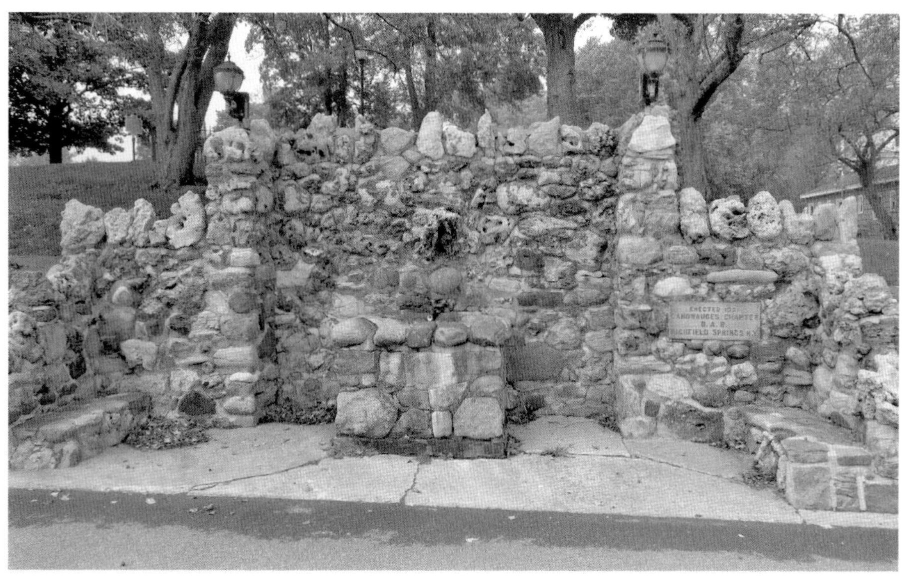

Sulphur Springs fountain, Richfield Springs. *Courtesy of the author.*

Today, Canadarago Lake at the village's tip remains a haven of recreation. Richfield Springs is one of those once-thriving gems circumvented by most people today in favor of the Thruway's speedy travel. Sharon Springs is another.

Sharon Springs

The town of Sharon, New York, dates to early German immigrants of the Mohawk Valley. Originally called New Dorlach, settlers migrating from Sharon, Connecticut, later changed the name. However, as New Dorlach, the village saw battle between the Americans and Tories. Growth was slow following the war, but even peacetime could not guarantee progress. Sharon Springs had to rely on its natural resources, just like Richfield Springs. Its mineral waters were the key.

The nineteenth-century resort age really was a new age for New York State, one that brought growth and magnificent architecture to these towns. Mineral waters used for commerce began in Sharon Springs in 1825 with David Eldredge, who owned a boardinghouse. The mineral springs were well known by 1841.

Connected via stagecoach, and later by railroad lines, bringing people from New York City and Boston, Sharon Springs became a major spa location. It had an average of more than ten thousand summer visitors for use of the baths. Some of America's iconic names came here to play, including the Vanderbilts, Roosevelts, Rockefellers and Oscar Wilde, who gave a lecture in 1882. Ulysses S. Grant also visited for brief stays. When the Erie Canal took traffic and commerce elsewhere, Sharon Springs remained viable, thanks to its spas. However, the spa era's end, and relocation of Route 20, put this bustling community to sleep. Much like the story of Sleeping Beauty, it seems to be waiting patiently to be awakened.

Eventually, Sharon Springs went the way of the era's many resort towns. The horse races and baths in Saratoga Springs slowly siphoned off the social set. Well-to-do Jewish families who were not welcome in Saratoga replaced the social elite, keeping Sharon Springs in business for a while longer. However, the glittering age was a time of competition. Soon, even Jewish patrons left for more modern facilities.

There was a brief period of beer production, with beer makers drawn by the region's hops. Nevertheless, Prohibition dried up sales of local hop harvests. Many beer companies went out of business.

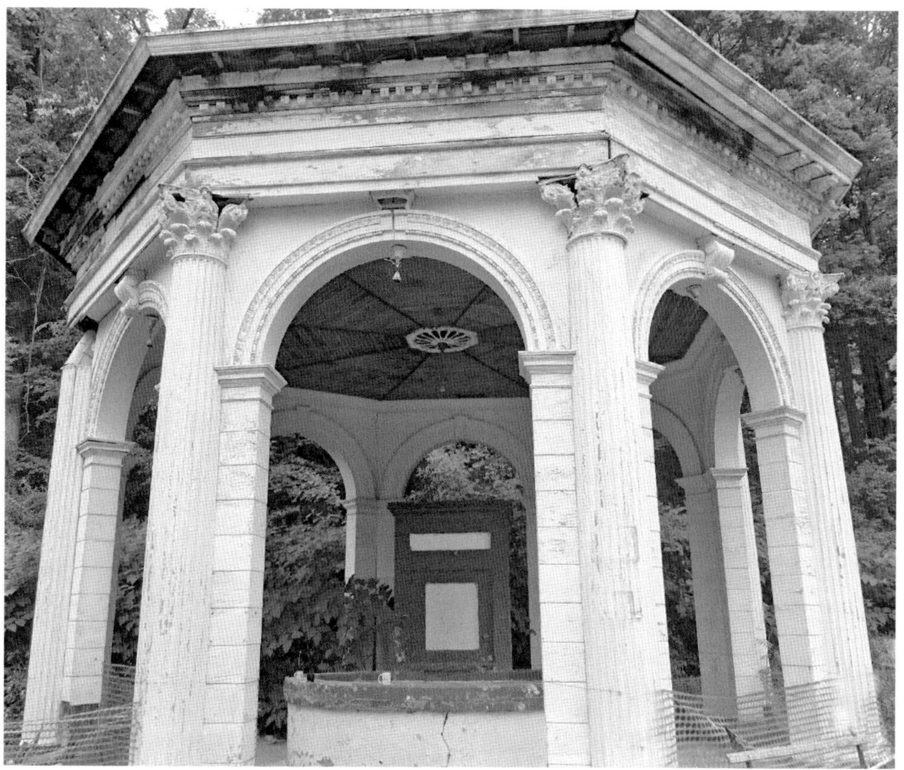

Pavilion Hotel Temple in Sharon Springs. *Courtesy of the author.*

Sharon Springs also had several self-catering boardinghouses that made it possible for people who could not afford pricey hotels to stay and take part in the local economy. These Jewish-operated boardinghouses were called kuchaleyans, meaning "cook's alone." This tradition more or less died out in 1960. Typical of these rooming houses, the Brustman House on Union Street remains from this period as a private family retreat.

The village did well again after World War II, when Holocaust survivors were given permission to use German reparations for medical treatments in the spas. Secular Jewish populations were replaced with Orthodox and Hassidic in the decades of the 1970s through the 1990s. The village became a weekend and holiday spot, later attracting businesspeople and sportsmen.

Sadly, New York State's Thruway put the last nail in Sharon Springs' coffin, sending most travelers past it without even blinking an eye. The once-thriving resort town is sparsely populated, even though it's been listed in the National Register of Historic Places since 1994 for its historic spa architecture.

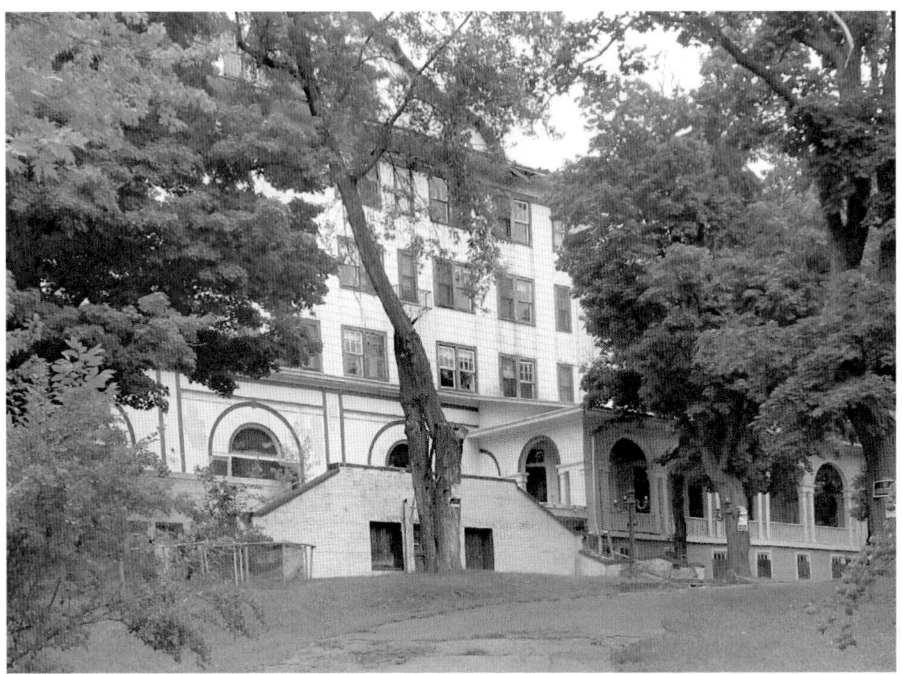

Addler Hotel in Sharon Springs. *Courtesy of the author.*

Perhaps it might yet awaken as architectural preservation takes place. The American is one of the earliest buildings to be restored as a hotel again. It was on this hotel's 1847 porch that Oscar Wilde gave regular readings. Natural gas companies have since been drawn to the Marcellus shale formation near the village's fringe, possibly ushering in another era for Sharon Springs.

One cannot help be drawn to the village's surrounding natural beauty in contrast to the massive architecture of the spa era, whose hotels and temples seem but apparitions. Sharon Springs feels like a ghost town, haunted by sounds of laughter and conversation on long hotel verandas in a summer breeze, echoing the eagerness of those hoping to be cured by its waters.

UTOPIAS AND PLAYGROUNDS OF THE RICH

Oneida Community and Sherrill, New York: "The Silver City"

Running parallel to the natural spring movement in New York State was the utopian movement, or Second Great Awakening, an era of religious fervor. It was a time of great change in America, which was turning from a wilderness into a country of immigrants and industry. There was no shortage of social issues in a once small, localized country. The utopian movement took hold in ways that would change societal landscapes again, and John Humphrey Noyes was instrumental at its infancy.

Noyes was born in Vermont in 1811. His father was a politician, and his cousin was U.S. president Rutherford B. Hayes. In 1831, at age twenty, Noyes experienced religious conversion in his own life. Noyes attended colleges where ministers of this movement often gravitated, receiving his license in ministry. The "Age of Perfectionism" was ushered in with a desire to live a simpler life. Noyes believed that man had to attain this state of perfectionism to receive God's blessings. He preached that heaven could be achieved on earth. Noyes, along with many others of the Great Awakening, felt one might best reach these religious goals by duplicating heaven on earth in self-sufficient communities. Those living in these communes were considered equals, with roles to play in support of the community.

However, Noyes's beliefs had a unique structure. In his ideal world, there was no marriage. Men and women were allowed to choose partners on a whim without stigma or a marriage license. Noyes insisted on methods for controlling birthrates, determining who could or could not become a parent. He started his first community in Vermont in 1840. However, due to his promiscuous teachings, he lost his minister's license. In 1847, Noyes's sexual ideologies forced his followers from Vermont. One year later, they founded Oneida Community in Oneida, New York.

As with any self-sufficient community, Oneida Community required an economy. It used its individual resources within the commune, dealing with the outside world for goods it could not produce. Inhabitants tried their hands at many different trades. Oneida Community members farmed and ran a blacksmith, sawmill and silk mill. They even dealt in beaver traps.

By 1881, followers had turned away from the open marriage doctrine set in place by Noyes in favor of conventional ideals. Productiveness in the community led to an accumulation of nearly $1 million. Rather than disband, community members used these monies to become a joint stock company as Oneida Community Limited. Today, we know them as Oneida Limited, makers of fine cutlery. After more than a century, the Oneida Company in Sherrill, New York, ceased all production in the United States, closing its doors in 2005.

Oneida Community Mansion House, built beginning in 1861, once housed its over three hundred members as one family. One can still tour and stay in this ninety-three-thousand-square-foot Victorian brick mansion that also affords an environment for weddings and other functions. It stands as a symbol of yet another fascinating story from our past.

Cazenovia: Owahgehaga (Where Yellow Perch Swim)

The town of Cazenovia was established along with five others prior to the formation of Madison County, although not incorporated until 1810. It covered a very large territory at one time; in fact, it encompassed what are now several small villages.

John Lincklaen, an agent of the Holland Land Company, founded Cazenovia in 1793, just three years after he arrived in the United States. The village is named after Theophilus Cazenove, a Dutch financier with the land company. John Lincklaen was his employee, owning land of his own on which he built his estate, Lorenzo. It still stands near Cazenovia Lake, around which the town is built.

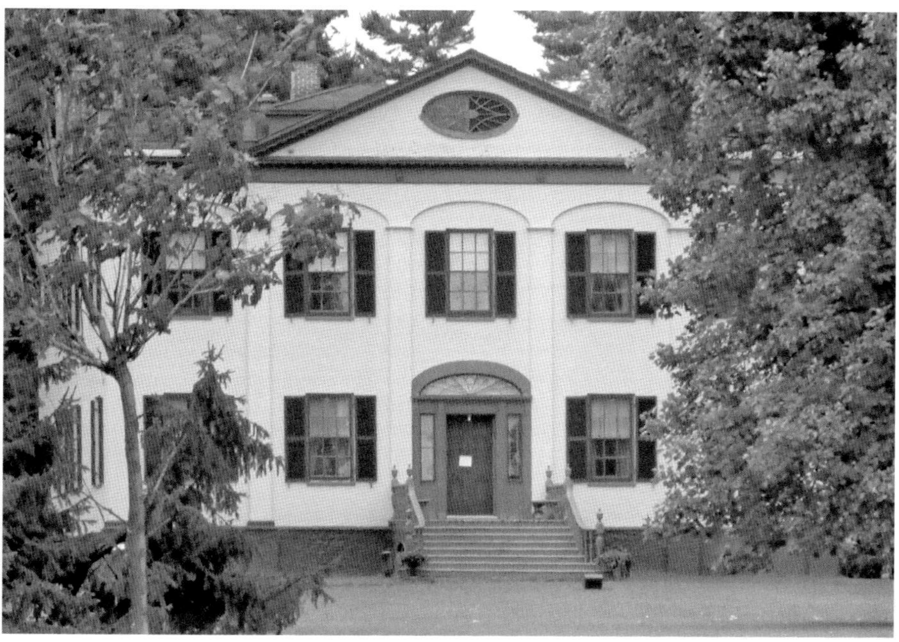

John Lincklaen's Lorenzo, Cazenovia. *Courtesy of the author.*

Lincklaen's work for the Holland Land Company was to sell lands in central New York purchased by his employer. Making good on this expectation, Lincklaen promised one hundred acres at $1.00 per acre to the first ten families buying land. He kept his word yet raised the price to $1.50 for anyone purchasing after the first ten.

These low prices attracted people who would rather take their chances in the wilderness than pay more in settled regions. Period documents state that the demand for these lands was so great the land company could not keep up. Many purchasers had to take their second or third choices, as others beat them to prime property. With demand came higher prices. Though at first no more than two dollars, prices rose as high as ten dollars per acre for some lots.

Two years after its founding, Lincklaen's agency was nearly devoid of further land to sell. Truth be told, quite a few settlers are said to have defaulted on their payments. Apparently, there were some whose motives were to conquer the wilderness and then move on to the next wild place without paying. These men were adventure seekers. The situation left lands open without buyers as settlers became disenchanted with the local economy. Roads were not yet suitable, so produce could not reach markets where it sold at a decent profit. As a result, Cazenovia had a small working class and an abundance of wealthy landowners who did not buy their land through the land agent. Instead, they shrewdly bought out contracts from settlers who had paid very little for their property.

Lincklaen knew most early Americans desired both religious and secular instruction. He also knew the value of settlers with religious morality. Therefore, when he laid out plots for sale, he set aside two lots of over one hundred acres for a church and school. As the settlement grew, he offered large lots to the first institution built in each of five districts. It is likely he sold that land to private citizens as profit saw fit, knowing settlers would build churches without his help.

The War of 1812 brought another peak period as many migrants decided to halt their journeys in Cazenovia rather than move on westward. Cazenovia afforded security when westward enterprise during the war seemed unstable. By the turn of the nineteenth century, not only had vacant lands been sold but also early residents had become established enough to finally pay down their debts.

However, Cazenovia, like most early settlements, had its economic slumps as well as advances. Even Lincklaen's good business sense could not control outside influences. Following the war, Lincklaen was ordered to sell off remaining holdings in Cazenovia so money could be diverted to rebuilding the fledgling nation. At this time, holdings had become stock shares, of which Lincklaen owned nearly two hundred. He was concerned that such an abrupt sale would mean lower prices at his own expense. Lincklaen sought a solution that was approved by the land company. He purchased the enterprise—a great idea that proved unprofitable for him. The company was more fortunate; it bailed out in time.

Postwar times were difficult on the region, as well as the country. In addition to these hardships, the government enticed settlers into the Mississippi Valley by offering low-priced land. Roads had improved, making these migrations easier. Furthermore, the Erie Canal drained the region of competitive markets. It became less expensive to transport goods by barge than overland. While this sounds like a good thing, for producers around Cazenovia, it meant they could no longer price their goods at reasonable profit margins. As such, Lincklaen never fully recovered his financial losses.

Today, Cazenovia is a thriving haven for vacationers. The lake region's limestone and dairy farming remain lucrative parts of local economy. The railroad and Route 20 are both responsible for its success, as is the

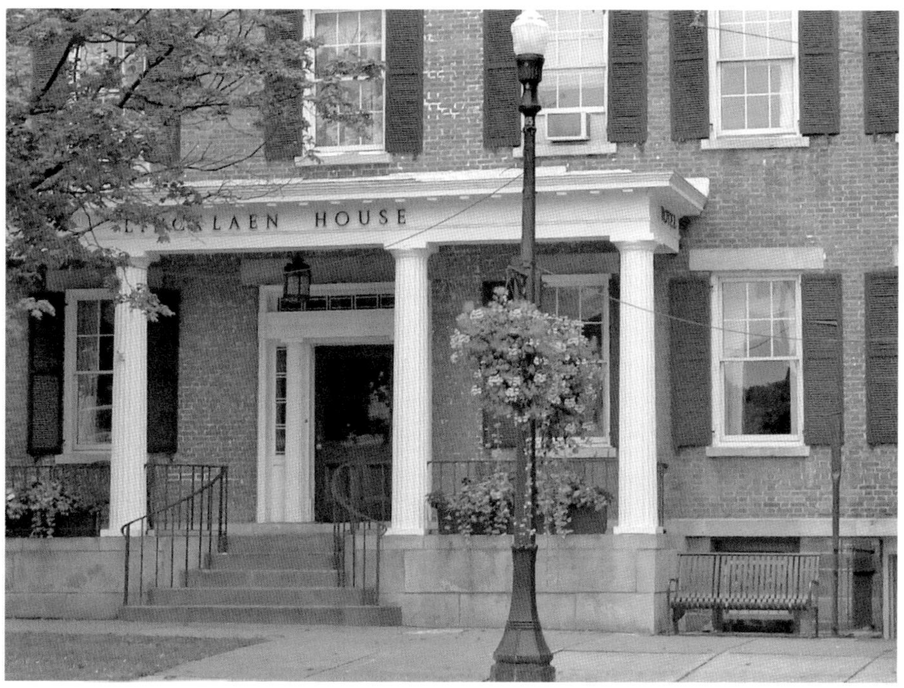

Lincklaen House in Cazenovia. *Courtesy of the author.*

lake that has drawn people for many decades, as well as the services required to keep them happy. These make up much of Cazenovia's businesses today. Many exquisite homes from the 1800s can still be seen. It is also the location of Cazenovia College, founded in 1824 as the second Methodist seminary in the United States and among the first colleges to be coeducational.

Cazenovia's history is inseparable from its founder. Even a hotel built in 1835 bears his name, Lincklaen House. Looking at this hotel, one sees the past. Little has changed in the building's design from a time when stagecoaches brought visitors from Washington, Philadelphia, New York City and elsewhere. The hotel served the likes of President and Mrs. Grover Cleveland and John D. Rockefeller. This gives us a very clear picture of those who traveled for pleasure in the nineteenth and early twentieth centuries—they were wealthy urbanites. Cazenovia is vital yet laid back and rural, still affording the solitude so many crave.

John Lincklaen and Lorenzo

Lincklaen's vision of his mansion began in 1803, at which time he already had a lakeshore home. When his lake house caught fire in 1807, Lincklaen stepped up construction. Learning from the fire, he used brick inside and out so the mansion would be fireproof. He moved his family in one year later, naming the estate Lorenzo.

In 1820, near the end of his life, with failing health and heavy debt, Lincklaen abandoned Lorenzo. He and his wife went to live in Cazenovia with his brother-in-law. When John passed two years later, his wife put the house up for sale. Nobody was interested in buying it. Her younger brother, Jonathan Ledyard, had taken over the land business, debt and all. Now he purchased the last of John Lincklaen's dreams for a mere $100. Mrs. Lincklaen moved back into the mansion with her brother's family, but in an odd twist, in 1826, she convinced Jonathon to sell the estate back to her for the same $100.

Lorenzo passed down through the family, becoming a summer home in 1871. It switched over to the Fairchild family through marriage when the previous Lincklaen resident died in 1894. That resident was Lincklaen Ledyard, who turned his name around to Ledyard Lincklaen to keep the Lincklaen name alive.

Many changes took place, with new innovations and the addition of a grounds keeper's cottage. The estate continued to pass through family hands, this time via Fairchild to Ledyard to Remington, all connected to Lincklaen through his wife's family, until no one was left. In 1968, Lorenzo was donated to the New York Historic Trust.

It is rare that we see an estate of this nature remain in one family line and then be entrusted as a legacy to the people. This might be attributed to one son in the Ledyard family who remained unmarried with a lifetime grant of residency in South Cottage on the estate. He lived until 1970.

Lorenzo survived five generations on the Lincklaen-Ledyard family tree.

Please Do Drink the Water: Skaneateles

Skaneateles Lake, meaning "long lake" in the Iroquois language, is one of the Finger Lakes. Its water is among the country's cleanest natural reserves, being pumped as tap water to many surrounding communities. This place was once a rich hunting and fishing ground for native peoples.

The first white men arriving at Skaneateles Lake might have been Moravian missionaries in 1750, although the village was not settled until after the Revolutionary War as part of the Military Tract. Surveyor Abraham A. Cuddeback was the first settler in 1794. Cuddeback brought his wife and eight children, their livestock and all their worldly goods on a journey that took over five weeks. This story of long, arduous travel was repeated as many courageous families settled New York State all the way to Buffalo.

Many name different men as the first settler. Some say it was John Thompson, who was first to receive land, though he did not occupy it until the early 1800s. Cuddeback leased his land from his employer, so he was late to own it. Another man, Elijah Bowen, purchased and resided immediately. Whoever was first, these men and their families left behind what was familiar to them, risking much to settle in the wilds.

The Seneca Turnpike was that portion of Routes 5 and 20 between "Bagg's Square" in Utica (Old Fort Schulyer) and Canandaigua. Its safer travel brought more pioneers and their skills. Skaneateles became a thriving town, which today is a tourists' mecca.

While early settlers had to cart their grains all the way to Utica to be ground, by 1798, Skaneateles had its first mill. Winston Day was the town's first merchant, and then James Porter built a tavern. They were followed by many businesses and homes. The settlers harnessed the lake water to drive various industries, including a woolen mill. The town also produced ironwork, machinery, sleighs, paper and bricks, along with dairy and grain on local farms.

Judge Jedediah Sanger of Oneida County, who purchased land in Skaneateles, invested heavily in the first mills and built a dam in 1797. Sanger was also instrumental in creating the Seneca Turnpike and a bridge over the lake outlet in 1800. His contributions helped further western expansion.

Sleigh production and repair would have been an important part of the early economy, as so many traveling westward preferred smooth, snow-covered roads. Cultivating teasel, a roadside weed to us today, became a significant economy for Skaneateles. This burr was used to raise the nap on wool. The mid- to late industrial age, through the beginning of World War II, brought production of canoes, motorboats and sailboats for wealthy vacationers.

In the early 1800s, most households still had spinning wheels to make yarn for knitting and weaving. Wheelwright, innovator and inventor Amos Miner is among Skaneateles's famous sons for his invention that improved on old-style spinning wheels. The idea for his accelerating wheel head came to him while

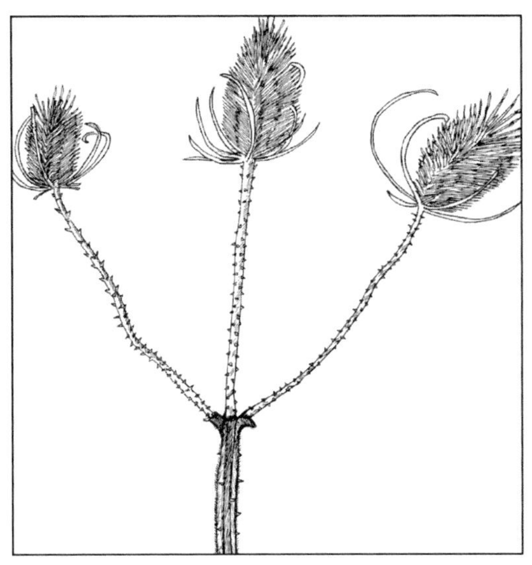

Producing teasel to raise the nap on wool became a lucrative industry in Skaneateles. *Courtesy of artist Alice Gerard.*

he was convalescing from an injury suffered clearing land. He gained his patent in 1803, and Miner's invention sold countrywide. In 1804, he bought land that included a mill.

The word in manufacturing success was diversity, so Miner built a factory for not only his wheel heads but other goods, too. After selling his land in 1805, he opened a new business with two other men. Again, he sold this business and opened a saw- and gristmill between Skaneateles and Otisco Lakes. With somewhat of a wandering soul, Amos Miner moved from Skaneateles to settle in Mottville, yet in all his endeavors, he continued to design and build his own machinery. Amos Miner was very much an example of the pioneering spirit that built this great nation.

Great Genesee Road, or Route 20, connected points west of Skaneateles with points east to Albany, making it an ideal stagecoach route. Isaac Sherwood, proprietor of Sherwood Inn, founded the first stagecoach line through the village. The Sherwood Inn, built in 1807, a way station for his stagecoach business, was located at the edge of a once massive cedar swamp. This exclusive restaurant and inn is still a stop for visitors.

Whether it was the lake's beauty or the rural proximity to larger cities, Skaneateles, like Cazenovia, attracted many well-to-do residents whose lakeside homes are mirrored in its waters. A far cry from early pioneers who struggled against nature's ever-changing temperament to build a new country, these wealthy settlers retired along the lake for its recreation and solitude.

Among the wealthy in Skaneateles were many who also contributed to the cause of freedom and the local economy. Skaneateles's founder, William J. Vredenburgh, was one such man.

Vredenburgh served as an officer in the military. He was paid for his service with land, which he sold to buy additional property. These dealings eventually brought him to Skaneateles with his wife and their six children in

1803. Here he purchased a house and land attached to it. Later, he bought unsold land held by Judge Sanger, and it was on that land that the village expanded. Vredenburgh also purchased twenty acres to build his future home, beginning construction in 1804. The great mansion was surrounded by pleasant gardens and was a spectacle in its day.

Unsatisfied that he had to travel to Marcellus to get his mail, Vredenburgh convinced the United States Postal Service to open a post office in Skaneateles. He was Skaneateles's first postmaster. When Vredenburgh died in 1813, his estate of several thousand acres was left to Daniel Kellogg. His mansion passed through several hands until it burned in 1872.

Nicholas Roosevelt, a member of the Roosevelt family, was an inventor. His most influential invention was the vertical paddle wheel for steamboats. There is no doubt about his financial contributions throughout the state. In 1809, Roosevelt combined efforts with Robert Fulton, bringing steamboats to the western waterways. After building and navigating the *New Orleans*, the steamboat that traveled the Ohio and Mississippi Rivers to New Orleans, Roosevelt filed and received a patent for his vertical paddle design. A legal battle ensued between Roosevelt and Fulton over who had actually created the design, but by the time the matter was settled, Roosevelt and his family had retired to Skaneateles. His days were spent blissfully there until his death in 1847.

The same year Nicholas Roosevelt came to Skaneateles, another inventor and canal builder moved in. His name was Richard DeZeng. His mansion is a Georgian Revival–style home on a rise overlooking beautiful Skaneateles Lake. Stories say he had it built in New York City, disassembled it, moved it to Skaneateles and reassembled it there. That would make it one of a

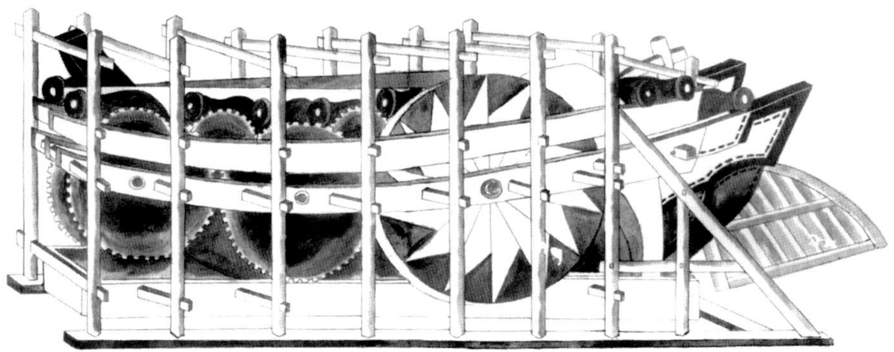

Paddle wheel mechanism of a side-wheel steamer. *Courtesy of the Library of Congress, Prints and Photographs Division.*

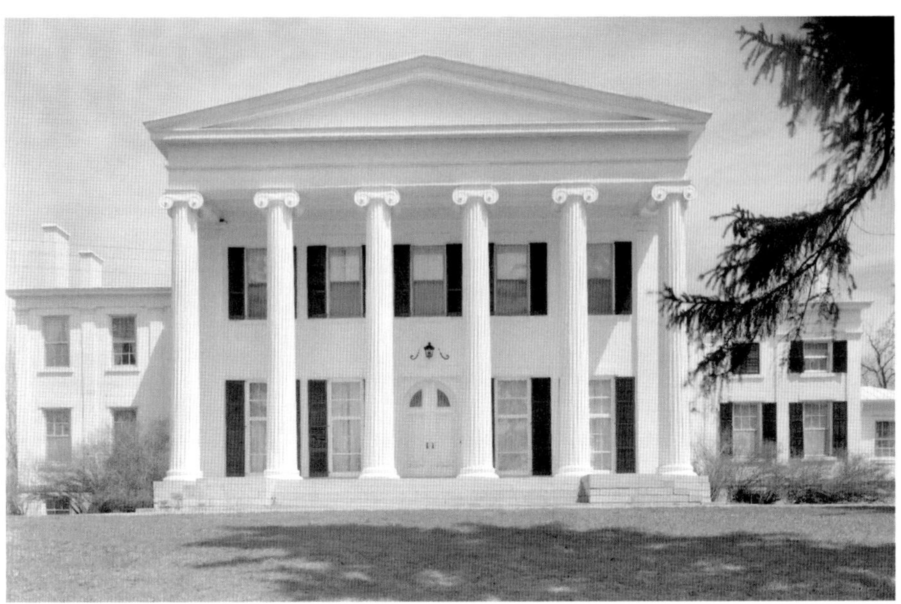

Front elevation, showing Ionic portico, Richard DeZeng House, West Lake Road, Skaneateles, Onondaga County, New York. *Courtesy of the Library of Congress, Prints and Photographs Division.*

kind in 1839 and very remarkable considering its size. In 1899, Samuel Montgomery Roosevelt purchased the twenty-five-room mansion and renamed it Roosevelt Hall. This stately home has had such visitors as Franklin D. Roosevelt and Robert Kennedy during his bid for the U.S. Senate. Robert Kennedy planned to buy the estate until deciding the dining room was too small. Roosevelt Hall was home to political royalty.

The only house designed by famed New York City architect Alexander Jackson Davis to remain in Onondaga County is the Gothic Revival home of Reuel Smith. Built between 1848 and 1852, this gingerbread-encrusted mansion is known as the Reuel E. Smith House or The Cove and was meant to break with the stiff-collared Greek style. Smith's contributions to Skaneateles were of the economic kind. He was a wealthy importer from Massachusetts who retired there.

As with many beautiful places in New York State, the peaceful atmosphere of Skaneateles Lake attracted those seeking a new way of life, and among them were the Quakers.

The Quakers, or Society of Friends, broke away from the Church of England. They spread throughout Great Britain and on to America with its

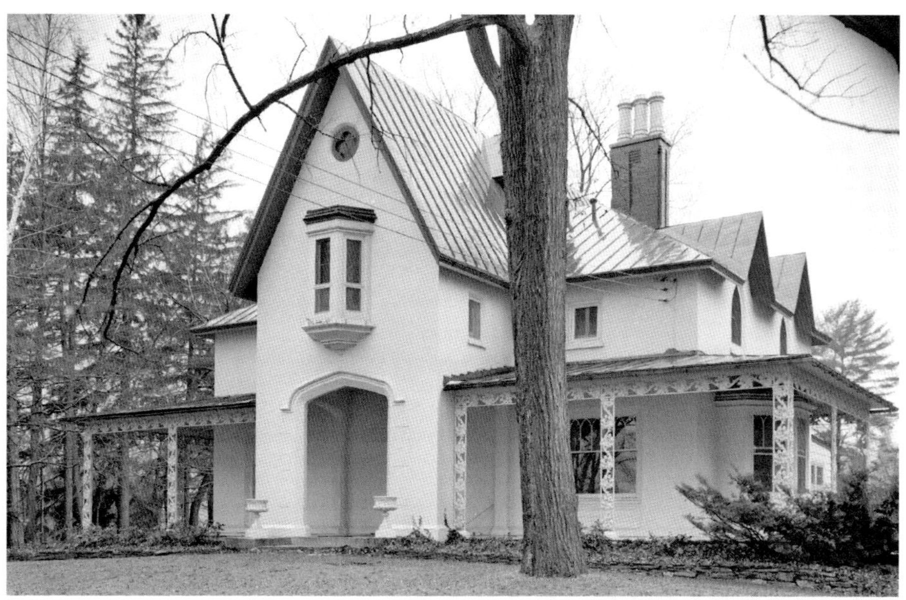

General view of east front and north side, Reuel Smith House, West Lake Road, Skaneateles, Onondaga County, New York. *Courtesy of the Library of Congress, Prints and Photographs Division.*

promise of hope and freedom, both personal and religious. They arrived on American shores as early as the 1680s.

In the 1700s, the Quakers instituted the idea of Quietism, a way of life that promoted reflection and a peaceful spirit, certainly something Skaneateles Lake could offer as one of several places they started communities. The lake's western shores became very settled by the Quakers. Their community in Skaneateles began about 1812 with a meetinghouse located near the octagon schoolhouse built by them as a girl's dormitory. The schoolhouse is a private residence today. Another meetinghouse was built on the farm of Richard Talcott after an internal split so that the community had both "Hicksites" and "Orthodox" Quakers. That meetinghouse was torn down in 1873, and yet another was raised. The Quakers were in Skaneateles to stay, and many became prominent citizens.

The Friends were active in the antislavery movement. One of their members, James Canning Fuller, from Great Britain, and his wife, Lydia, were very influential. Their home was a station on the Underground Railroad. The Fullers even went so far as to travel to slave states to buy slaves, including entire families, and then brought them north to set them

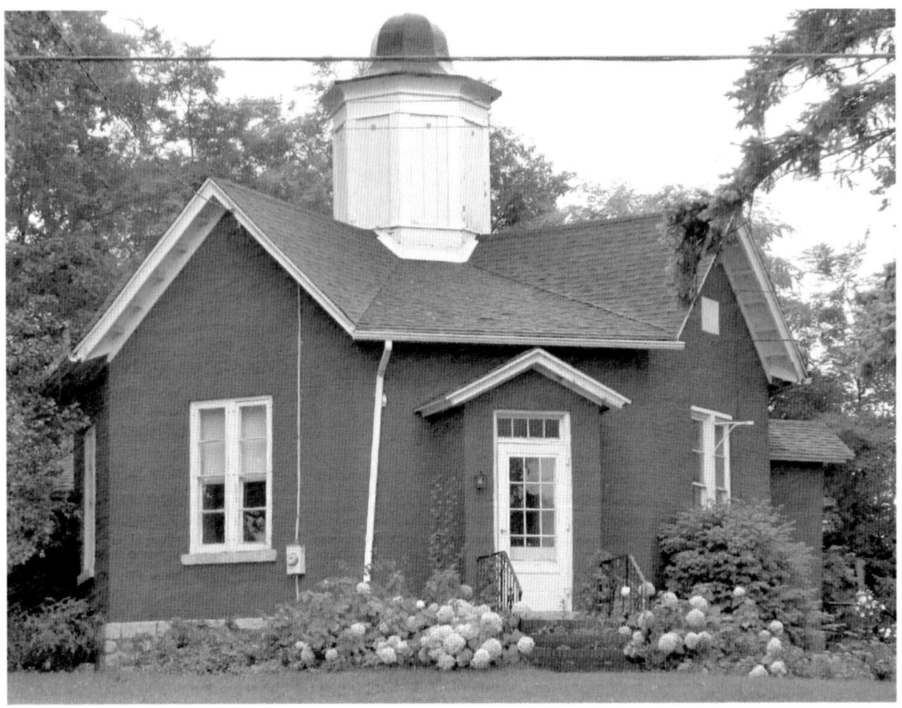

Quaker octagon schoolhouse, private residence, Skaneateles. *Courtesy of the author.*

free. One documented case was in 1841, when they purchased a family of seven in Kentucky. This was a dangerous undertaking. They truly risked their lives in this effort, more than once coming close to being mobbed. James was also co-founder of the British-American Institute, a school in Canada for fugitive slaves.

Thanks mainly to the Society of Friends, Skaneateles matched even Syracuse in its antislavery activity. This is remarkable considering Skaneateles was once a slaveholding village where even Frederick Douglass feared to enter.

Travelers can find a Quaker Cemetery on Benson Road in the town of Skaneateles. James Canning Fuller was buried in the Quaker section of Lake View Cemetery in 1847.

> *Much of this change was wrought by that fast, faithful, and noble friend of the slave, now gone to his rest, James Canning Fuller, who in early anti-slavery times was several times mobbed on account of his abolition*

> *principles and practice. But he is now gone to his rest. It was sad to be there without his presence, to cheer and encourage me in the good work to which he was devoted; yet it was grateful, to perceive that what he achieved lived after him.*
> *—Frederick Douglass, on his visit to Skaneateles in 1849.*

As with Oneida, Skaneateles had, for a short time, its own utopian community. These communities are collectively considered part of the Burned-Over District that stretched across central and western New York, regions highly influenced by the Evangelical movement and difficult to convert.

Skaneateles Community was formed in 1843 by the Society for Universal Inquiry and Reform. It established itself on 350 acres, where it operated a farm and some small factories. The community had approximately one hundred members and did very well financially until internal struggles and a negative view of its social practices shut it down after three years. Some locals referred to the community as "No God."

Another utopian movement that took place in Skaneateles was Community Place, formed in 1830. This community was housed in a building known as Frog Pond, currently on the Historic Register. It was a Fourierist commune for three years and fairly successful. Fourierism was based on the philosophy of Charles Fourier, a French social theorist who advocated a self-sufficient society. This meant that people should be naturalistic and free of governmental restraint.

In a country just free of its bondage to England and in search of its future, these ideologies gathered followers, even if not always accepted by communities at large. The spirit of these communes and their contributions to New York State's history remain ever present.

ON THE ROAD TO FREEDOM

What is it that draws like-minded people or similar ideas to a location? Is it migration of ideas, proximity and access? Lay lines? Vortexes? Whatever the cause, the area within a few miles of Syracuse and Skaneateles has drawn on the idea of "freedom for all." Be it religion, the plight of slaves or women's rights, there is definitely a mass of such communities located at the heart of central New York.

All Aboard the Freedom Train: Auburn, New York

Auburn is located about thirty miles south of Syracuse, midway between Skaneateles and Seneca Falls. It was home to one of the antislavery movement's most significant mothers, Harriet Tubman. Miss Tubman was responsible for helping over seventy slaves into lives of freedom. She also served as a Civil War spy and nurse and fought for women's rights.

She is disputably quoted as saying, "Children, if you are tired, keep going; if you are scared, keep going; if you are hungry, keep going; if you want to taste freedom, keep going." The tone was right for this time of nation building.

Harriet Tubman set out to succeed and expected that same moxie from those she helped. She could not afford her charges to fail and face certain punishment or death by attempting to return to the places they had escaped. She could not allow her mission to fail because of one man's fear or weakness under the lash. She always urged them onward. Abolitionist John Brown called Harriet "General Tubman," and rightfully so. She was a great leader at a time when neither "Negroes" nor women had a voice many would hear.

Born into slavery around 1820 in Dorchester, Maryland, under the name of Araminta Rose, Harriet Rose, as she came to be called when she turned eleven, knew full well the slave's harsh life. Beatings, lashings, hunger, cold—as a child, she experienced it all. She was put to work at age six on loan by her master to a couple for their weaving work.

When Harriet turned twenty-five, her name changed again, this time to Harriet Tubman when she married a free black man. She herself remained a slave but dreamed of being liberated. She often talked to her husband of it. He was content where he was and would not support her dreams. In 1849, Harriet escaped bondage, both of her spirit and of her marriage. Thus began her own travels on the Underground Railroad. Abolitionists gave her directions that took her to Philadelphia. Once there, this brave and selfless woman worked to make money to help set others free.

In 1850, following passage of the Fugitive Slave Act that made it illegal to aid escaped slaves, the codes of the Underground Railroad became more secretive. Slaves were sent to Canada instead of just into Northern states. This increased the danger to all, but especially to people like Harriet, who was herself an escaped slave. There was a high price on her head. Harriet Tubman was a wanted fugitive. Even so, she made many trips to dangerous Southern locations and into Canada as a conductor.

The Society of Friends, known antislavery activists, had taken up residence in and around Auburn, New York. In addition, Auburn was home to U.S. senator and former New York State governor William Seward. Around 1850, Harriet befriended Seward and his wife. The Sewards, along with local Quakers, became stationmasters, helping many of Harriet's charges find homes. The Sewards helped Harriet's own niece when Harriet sent her to them. In 1857, they provided a home for Harriet's parents, whom she brought from Saint Catherines, Canada. Eventually, Harriet was able to purchase this home from them for a small amount, making it her base.

Though Harriet Tubman's house no longer stands, the site of the home where the "Moses of Her People" lived and died is owned by AME Zion Church. It sits as a memorial to her remarkable life and great work. What can be seen on the site is another of Harriet's endeavors built following the Civil War—a home for the aged.

The home of William Seward, who also served as secretary of state in the Lincoln-Johnson administration, can still be viewed. Seward is said to have

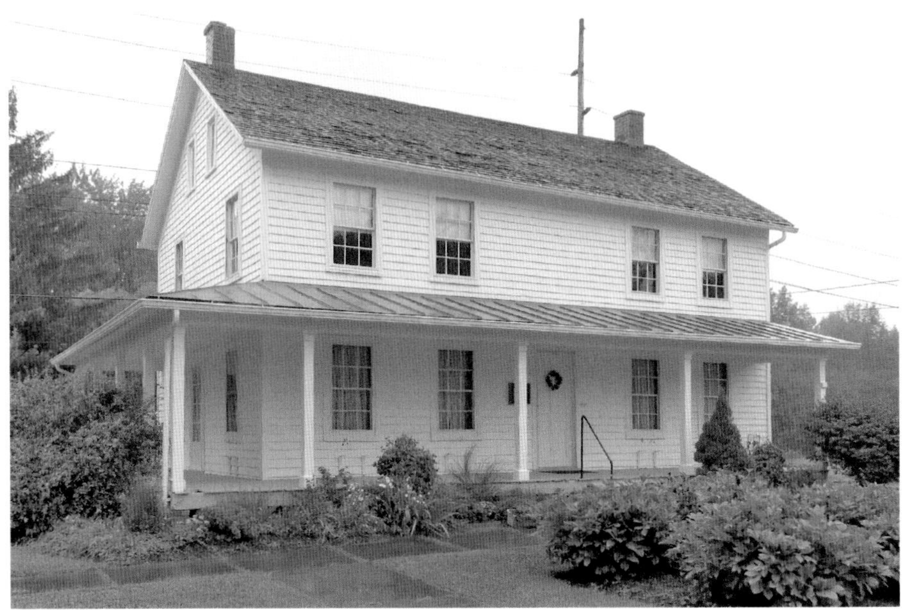

Harriet Tubman's home for the aged. *Courtesy of the author.*

led the way in the Alaska Purchase. His work in helping Harriet Tubman and keeping a nation from foreign influence at a time it was divided are amazing accomplishments.

Long before Harriet Tubman's arrival, or that of William Seward, Auburn in Cayuga County was Iroquois territory. John L. Hardenbergh was a veteran of the Sullivan Campaign. Settling near the Owasco River with an infant daughter and two slaves, Hardenbergh is credited with founding Auburn in 1793.

The original name, Hardenbergh's Corners, was changed to Auburn in 1805, when it became the county seat, one year before the founder's death. The village grew, as many did, with the Erie Canal in 1825. While the canal did not run through the town, it was only five miles away, greatly increasing goods shipped.

Auburn was the seat of the Auburn Theological Seminary, which closed in 1939. It was considered one of the United States' best. However, the only buildings remaining are Welch Memorial Hall and Willard Memorial Chapel, which was completely decorated by Louis Comfort Tiffany. The chapel is the only completely Tiffany-designed chapel still in existence.

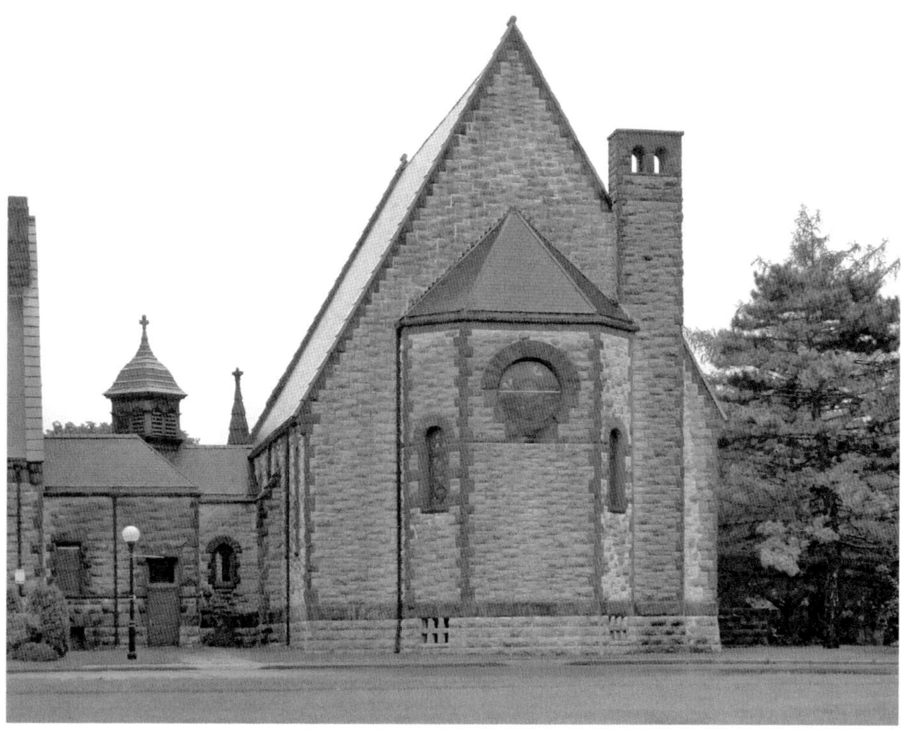

Willard Chapel exterior. *Courtesy of the author.*

Auburn Prison set a new standard of treatment for prisoners known as the Auburn System. The system was utilized in many other prisons of the day. Controversial, this system charged people a fee to view inmates in their daily activities. The electric chair, invented by Buffalo, New York dentist Alfred Southwick, was first used at Auburn in 1890. In 1901, the assassin who killed President William McKinley was executed in the prison. While it certainly no longer uses the Auburn System, the prison is still a maximum-security facility.

Considered the best-preserved Cayuga village site, Auburn's Fort Hill Cemetery is listed as a historical landmark. Besides being the sixteenth-century hill fortification for the Cayugas against rival tribes, it is the burial site of many notables, including William Seward and Harriet Tubman.

Seneca Falls: It's a *Wonderful Life*

West of Auburn, New York, on Routes 5 and 20 is Seneca Falls, sometimes called the "Gateway to the Finger Lakes." Water was and continues to be central to Seneca Falls and its economy. Cayuga and Seneca Lakes are connected to the Erie Canal via the Seneca Canal, which was built in 1818. The Finger Lakes and hills act in combination to create a perfect climate for grape growing. They also afford recreation for residents and visitors. The Seneca River now forms portions of the new Erie Canal running through the great Montezuma Swamp, a wildlife preserve.

Though settled following the Revolutionary War, the town did not form until after the Erie Canal was built in 1828. Like most canal towns, Seneca Falls grew as a result of the people and goods easily transported from Albany to Buffalo and back again.

Seneca Falls, called *Shasoonse*, meaning "swift waters," was once territory of the Cayugas. A portion of the town was a native reservation for those who returned following the war. During the war, however, Cayuga villages were destroyed in the Sullivan Campaign. Seneca Falls was also within the Military Tract.

Many early settlers came out of Sullivan's Campaign. Soldiers marching with Sullivan were inspired by the region's beauty and potential bounty. The earliest known settlers arrived in 1787 to claim veteran lots. The area was at that time known as Mynderse Mills after one landowner, Wilhelmus Mynderse.

Mynderse was actually more than a landowner. He held one-fifth interest in the Bayard Land Company, which in turn owned regional Military Tract lots and also controlled waterpower rights. His own allotment comprised over six hundred acres. Mynderse, the company land agent for thirty years, settled there permanently in 1795. He built a home that doubled as his office. He also built the customary grist- and sawmills.

Although many village founders certainly created wealth for themselves, including Wilhelmus Mynderse, they also gave back much to their communities. Mynderse's contributions continued in the form of additional mills and businesses, from cloth fulling to actual sales of merchandise. Mynderse served in the militia beginning in 1801. Mynderse Academy, part of the public school system, was built on lands he supplied, as was the town park. He donated a house to the library association for its early use. Later, Mynderse's son Edward continued in his father's footsteps, building two large brick homes. One was his own beautiful mansion, currently inhabited by the historical society and, many say, the ghost of a previous owner.

The village name was changed upon incorporation in 1831 to honor the waterfall at that location on the Seneca River. It was around the waterfall and rapids that the Seneca Canal was built, making transportation more accessible. Prior to this time, it was the waterfall that powered the mills and factories. In fact, with this local water power, Seneca Falls became the world's third-largest flour producer. One can definitely see the pattern of how New York State's waterways created settlements that in turn helped the entire state to succeed.

A name found when studying the state's industrial history is one that begins in Auburn, New York, settles in Seneca Falls and finally lands as a key figure in Lockport, New York. That name is Birdsall Holly.

Though little is known of his private life, and rumors abound about his personality, we do know that Birdsall Holly was drawn to Seneca Falls from his home in Auburn to take employment as a mechanic in one of Mynderse's mills. Birdsall Holly, or perhaps a son by the same name, as some reports suggest, was extremely fascinated with water and how it could be put into service. He developed a hydraulics system that led to the invention of the fire hydrant; the hydraulic raceway in Lockport, New York; a manufacturing company; steam heating; and over 150 patents in his lifetime, more even than Thomas Edison. As to his work in Seneca Falls, Holly partnered in the Silsby Company, also called the "Island Works" because it was located on a five-acre island on Seneca River. After Holly's move to Lockport, Silsby was taken over by Seabury Gould, who founded Gould Pumps, manufacturing the first cast-iron pump.

Some say Seneca Falls inspired Bedford Falls in the beloved Christmas tale *It's a Wonderful Life*, starring Jimmy Stewart. They hold a festival every year. But Seneca Falls is more than the quintessential American town; it is also the place that launched the women's rights movement.

The road to freedom can mean different things to many people, whether it is a new life free from bondage, freedom from toil made easier through invention or a life of adventure ensured because one can travel freely from place to place. For Seneca Falls, it meant a woman's right to rule her own life, taking an active role in what happens in her community and country with the right to vote.

Elizabeth Cady Stanton, an organizer for the Women's Rights Convention, was born in Johnstown and lived in Seneca Falls, as did Amelia Bloomer, whose ideas on "appropriate" attire for women also made a splash in the form of "bloomers." Amelia Bloomer was encouraged to write for her husband's newspaper, the *Seneca Falls County Courier*. She eventually formed her own paper.

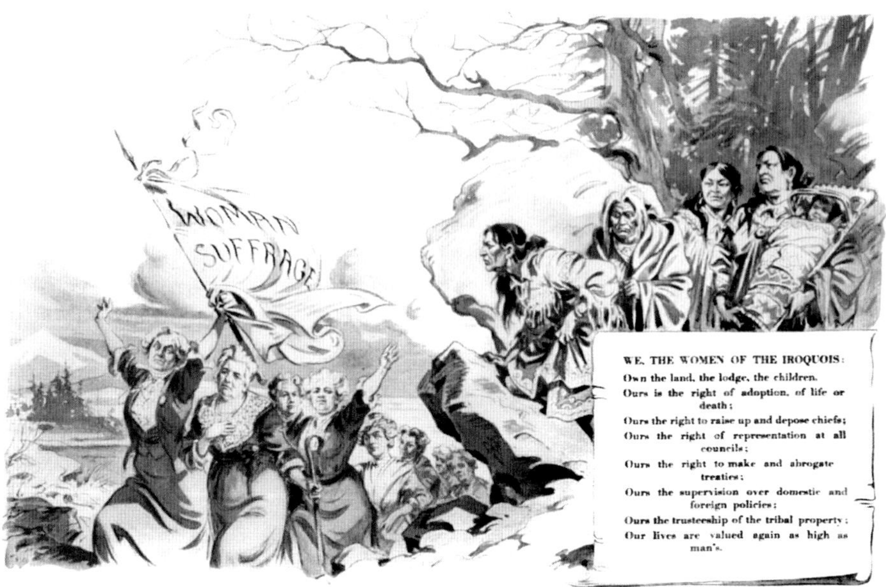

Women's suffrage: savagery to "civilization." *Courtesy of the Library of Congress, Prints and Photographs Division.*

The *Lily* was the first women's newspaper in the country. It published articles that encouraged new thought, from marriage law reform to higher education for women. Bloomer also believed women should be able to own and operate motor vehicles. Autos and "bloomers" meant newfound mobility for women.

Women with their own newspapers, wearing comfortable clothing, carrying signs, marching in the streets, leaving families to attend a convention of women—these things were considered unacceptable, until these women and their followers led the way. However, long before American women gained their rights, Iroquois women were already established as leaders, and it was on their ideals that much of the women's rights movement was built:

> *We the women of the Iroquois:*
> *Own the land, the lodge, the children.*
> *Ours is the right of adoption, of life, or death;*
> *Ours the right of representation at all councils;*
> *Ours the right to make and to* [abrogate] *treaties;*
> *Ours the supervision over domestic and foreign policies;*
> *Ours the trusteeship of tribal property;*
> *Our lives are valued again as high as man's.*

Seneca Falls gave birth to female leaders in the temperance and abolitionist movements as well. One such woman was Abby Kelly, a Quaker who showed little fear in addressing slavery openly in public forums in the faces of men and the church. A woman of some means, Kelly used her own money to help fund the antislavery movement. She spoke at conventions and gatherings throughout New England, later joining the women's rights movement as well.

The roads widened from native trails became roads widened with opportunity. They paved the way to the westernmost parts of the nation and to a brighter future for those previously disenfranchised. *That* is quite a legacy, and Seneca Falls led the way for women.

THE FINGER LAKES REGION

Waterloo: Birthplace of Memorial Day

Waterloo was the site of Skoi-Yase, a Cayuga village (circa 1500). The native name means "flowing water" and was located near the rapids of Seneca River. It was burned during the Sullivan Campaign. Samuel Bear was the first to settle and build in 1792. Waterloo's industrial history is rich, and the village was the site of planning for the first Women's Rights Convention. Perhaps it is most famous for giving birth to our national holiday, Memorial Day.

The idea for honoring America's fallen came from a druggist named Henry C. Welles. He felt we should praise living veterans but also place memorials on the graves of those who never made it home again. Is it any wonder he had this revelation? This was in 1865, following the Civil War, the country's bloodiest conflict. Welles took his idea to General John B. Murray, and the two men formed a committee. Waterloo held its first village-wide celebration on May 5, 1866. Memorial Day remembrances quickly spread to other villages, and by 1868, most were holding their festivities on May 30. Yet it would be a century later when New York State fully proclaimed the holiday. Congress eventually passed a resolution in which Waterloo is noted as the village where it all began. President Lyndon B. Johnson made it official with his signature on May 26, 1966:

Resolved that the Congress of the United States, in recognition of the patriotic tradition set in motion one hundred years ago in the Village of Waterloo, NY, does hereby officially recognize Waterloo, New York as the birthplace of Memorial Day…

Geneva: "Lake Trout Capital of the World"

Geneva rests in two counties, Ontario and Seneca, and did not incorporate until the early 1800s. Although white settlers came after the Revolutionary War, ancient tribes are known to have been there as early as 3500 BC. As with much of the wilderness interior, Jesuits were the first white men to visit in 1654. Today, the region is once more home to the Cayugas and Senecas, though their history was forever altered by the white man's conflicts. Knowing Geneva's critical location, the British created a stronghold here against the French. It was later fortified against the Americans. The Iroquois Nation was split in the process.

Geneva, located on the northern tip of Seneca Lake, the deepest of the Finger Lakes, overlays what was once the Seneca capital of Kanadasaga. Though never a fort, John Butler did build a barracks and storehouse here. This barracks sent out many raiding parties against American settlers. British-allied Indians left Kanadasaga for Oriskany and Cherry Valley from this barracks. In retaliation, General Sullivan left nothing standing, neither home nor harvest, in 1779.

One of the area's most famous residents was Horatio Jones. Born in Pennsylvania, he joined the military in 1781. Along with many in his regiment, Jones was captured during an Indian skirmish. Captives were taken to Nunda, New York, close to what is today Letchworth State Park. After heroically running the gauntlet, legend has it that Jones kept running—right into the longhouse of those who would later adopt him. Jones is said to have overcome every obstacle placed before him, from threats of death to hand-to-hand combat with rivals in the tribe. His captivity lasted until a treaty was signed between the newly formed United States and the Iroquois Confederacy in 1784. He was New York State's equivalent of Daniel Boone. No doubt, Horatio Jones had other adventures, but the first time his name shows up again is in 1786, when he settled in Waterloo, New York. After hunting and trading for one year, Jones moved closer to present-day Geneva. He later met his wife in Schenectady, bringing her to live in his cabin, where they started a family. Jones's story is reminiscent of *Drums Along the Mohawk*, in which a frontiersman meets his new bride in Albany and takes her to live in his cabin in the valley wilderness.

Jones, his wife and their three children remained at Kanadasaga (Geneva) until 1789, when they moved all their worldly goods, including cattle, to Leicester, New York. Horatio Jones was one of Leicester's earliest settlers as well. George Washington named him an Indian interpreter.

Following the war, a few traders and speculators infiltrated the Finger Lakes region. They set up their operations in Geneva on what is today known as Exchange Street. Their dealings were not sanctioned, giving rise to a notorious company called the Leasee Company. Members of this group stalled negotiations between the government and the Indians while trading with the Indians for all the supplies and liquor they could handle. This handful of Hudson Valley politicians and renegade British-allied Indians hoped to convince other settlers to vote for secession from the state. Furthermore, the illicit company is said to have duped the Indians into a deal for use of all Iroquois lands for a total of 999 years, a common lease practice meaning "for life." Leaseholders included Joseph Brant and John Butler, now outlaws who hoped their leases would be legalized. Their plan was foiled by the Fort Stanwix treaty and the Preemption Line agreement.

Much of the uncertainty over landownership stemmed from disputes between Massachusetts and New York, both having received charters from England. Until this problem was solved, no pioneer could legally settle on disputed lands. The Preemption Line divided lands in western New York from eastern lands held by Massachusetts via the Treaty of Hartford. This treaty stated that Massachusetts could buy lands west of the Preemption Line from the Indians for resale, while New York would govern those lands. Stories suggest that the Leasee Company had its own lines of demarcation in mind. Certainly, it seemed to ignore the law. It was easy to cast doubt over exactly where the Preemption Line was located and easier still to buy off surveyors and politicians.

Beyond obvious land fraud, settling Geneva was like settling other villages along Routes 5 and 20 in that so many began as private lots granted to soldiers in the Military Tract. It is astounding when one imagines how a city today was once land owned by an individual. One such early landowner was Revolutionary War hero Lieutenant Colonel Seth Reed, who fought at Bunker Hill. He moved his family to Geneva in 1790. Reed formed a land company with another man, Peter Ryckman. Reed and Ryckman owned over sixteen thousand acres, of which Reed owned two thousand for himself.

Reed's holdings comprised much of the village's southern portion, although Geneva was not yet incorporated. Reed and Ryckman eventually found themselves in competition with the Leasee Company.

Fraud and debates over where the Preemption Line actually lay were plentiful. Quite possibly, Reed's and Ryckman's lands lay outside what they originally believed were the legal limits. The line might actually have cut Geneva in half. In the end, titles held by the two men proved to also have been sold or given to another, and another and another. In other words, they were fraudulent or illegal. The true owner proved to be none other than Charles Williamson, land agent for Pulteney Associates. Reed finally decided to move his family to Erie, Pennsylvania, where they became among the first to call it home.

Even the Phelps and Gorham Company, another land-purchasing agency, found itself embroiled in disputes over delineations. It believed lands it purchased included Geneva, where it wanted to set up its headquarters, only to be told the area already belonged to the Leasee Company. Instead, Phelps and Gorham moved eastward to Canandaigua, becoming the first American-owned land company.

Nobody really knows if the land dealings were fraudulent due to faulty equipment, too much alcohol consumption on the job or just simple error. Regardless, a city rose on the banks of Seneca Lake in the fertile Finger Lakes region.

Pulteney Association, a group of European investors, included a baronet and Scottish lawyer, Sir William Pulteney, who was said to be the wealthiest man in Great Britain. The company resettled the area around Geneva in 1793. Pulteney's partners were William Hornby, one-time governor of Bombay (now Mumbai), and Patrick Colquhoun, a Scottish merchant. They purchased much of the land in what is considered central New York, making for a powerful endeavor. Their holdings are said to have been as large as six million acres, which included lumber, mineral and other natural resources found in abundance at that time. Pulteney's lands are called the Pulteney Purchase or Genesee Tract.

First official mention of Geneva as a village took place thirteen years later, in April 1806, when New York State granted it status. Even so, locals were already calling their settlement Geneva as early as 1788. How the village actually received its name is disputed. The name is said to have come from a Swiss engineer in honor of Geneva, Switzerland. There is no real record of this. What we do know is that aforementioned Charles Williamson was crucial in creating the city. Williamson, a Scotsman working for Pulteney, fell in love with the region. He inspired building and enterprise, as well as ideas for regulating how buildings and open spaces were laid out to make the most of the lake's view. The Geneva Hotel was one such building backed by Williamson.

Even though the village's population continued to grow, as did its commerce, Geneva did not gain recognition in business until the introduction of the railroad. Geneva's manufacturing included breweries, carriage makers, brickyards, foundries, machine shops, mills, tanneries, a yeast factory, cereals, an optics company and many others. However, it was the nursery business of the late nineteenth and early twentieth centuries that established Geneva's future.

Melting glaciers left the Finger Lakes with rich soils perfect for raising crops. Many early settlers came from New England and Virginia, leaving lands that had either been overfarmed or were not fertile to begin with. Geneva was a place that offered these pioneers a new opportunity to prosper. In fact, much of the earliest wealth in Geneva came from the soil. These pioneers made Geneva's nursery industry one to be rivaled. It is reported that almost the entirety of Geneva, Seneca and Phelps was one massive nursery.

A nursery near Waterloo held a vast orchard of various fruit trees. Another west of Geneva had nine hundred acres, of which four hundred were orchards or ornamental trees. There were many others nearly as large, all growing trees, plants and flowers.

One of the most well-known nurserymen who came out of this age was Geneva's Otto Stern, the creator of Miracle-Gro. Stern advertised in the *New York Times* that one could order a plant from his nursery in Geneva and have it shipped to California—a pioneering idea in its day.

Following World War II, it was the many foundries on Geneva's lakefront that kept the city alive. Today, it is wine growing, the waterways and Hobart and Smith Colleges that support the economy.

Of note is William Smith's connection to the college and the nursery industry, again showing how one man can influence the future. He and his brother immigrated to America from England in the 1800s, founding a nursery business in Geneva. William later organized the Standard Optical Company and was director of the First National Bank. He endowed Smith College, willing his mansion and observatory to Hobart. Today, an opera house and observatory also bear his name.

A story about Geneva would not be complete without at least a short mention of magnificent Belhurst Castle. Once the site of a Seneca village where the Six

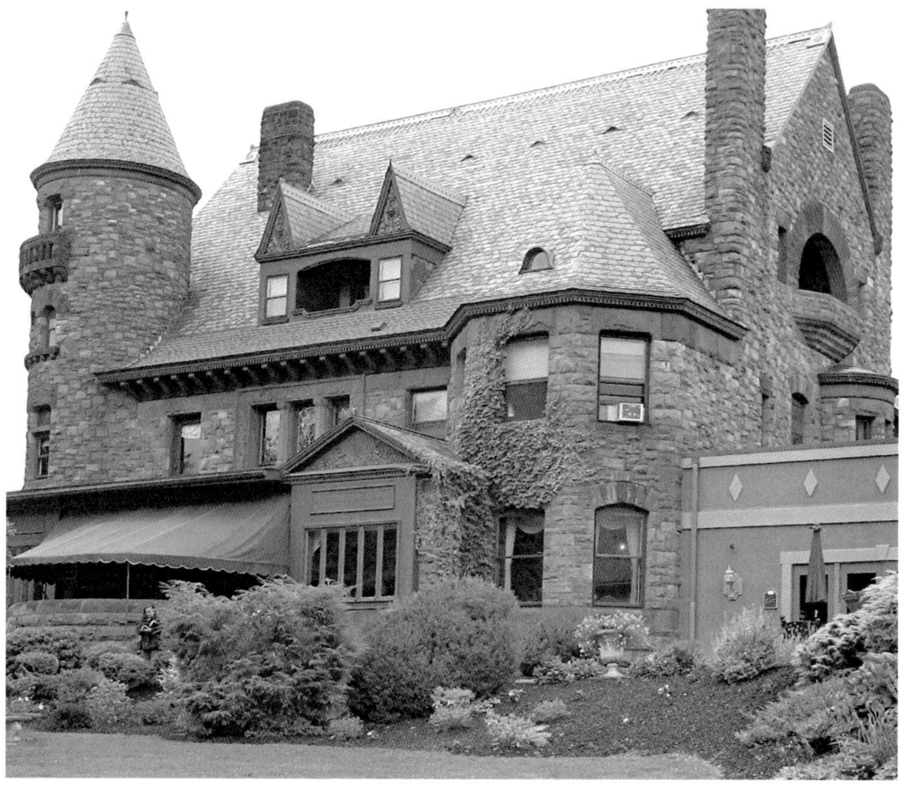

Belhurst Castle. *Courtesy of the author.*

Nations held council, this property has a rich history all its own. Sold during the years following the Revolution, it has gone through several transformations, from being the first glass factory west of Albany to home of an English lawyer who called it "The Hermitage." It is also the site of the death of an embezzler who married his stepmother. He died of blood poisoning from a wound. A strip of the property was sold to the railroad, and yet another piece became a cemetery. The main portion of the land was vacant for years, serving as a picnic grove for locals until 1885, when it was sold again to a New York socialite, Mrs. Harron. Shortly after purchase, she divorced her husband, remarried, tore down the old "hermitage" and began building her mansion. After her death, the castle became a speakeasy and gambling hall. Is it any wonder that this luxury hotel is considered haunted, complete with the resident ghost of the White Lady? Whether the White Lady is the ghost of an opera singer who died at the inn or the disgruntled wife of a speakeasy patron as some suggest, she might just as easily be a ghost reminding us of our storied past.

Canandaigua: Ganondagan or Kanandarque (The Chosen Spot)

The Seneca foothold in Canandaigua is so old that their ancestors, the Owascos, had a village, today marked as a state historical site. Later, Canandaigua was built on what had been Ganondagan, a significant Seneca village burned by Denonville.

The first white settlers arrived in 1789 after Phelps and Gorham established Canandaigua as their headquarters. It was here in 1794 that an important treaty was signed: the Treaty of Canandaigua, which sued for peace between the United States and the Six Nations. In addition, the treaty secured Iroquois land rights in New York State, as well as the boundaries established by Phelps and Gorham. This treaty was signed by some of the most well-known names in Iroquois history—Red Jacket, Handsome Lake, Corn Planter and Little Beard. Horatio Jones from Geneva was one of four interpreters present.

As significant to white settlers as to the natives, Canandaigua became the seat of Ontario County, then encompassing all of western New York's present thirteen counties. As a center for the legal system, it was here that leaders from the infamous Fenian Brotherhood, which attempted to hold Canada hostage until the English left Ireland, were sent from Buffalo upon their capture. Most noteworthy was women's rights activist Susan B. Anthony,

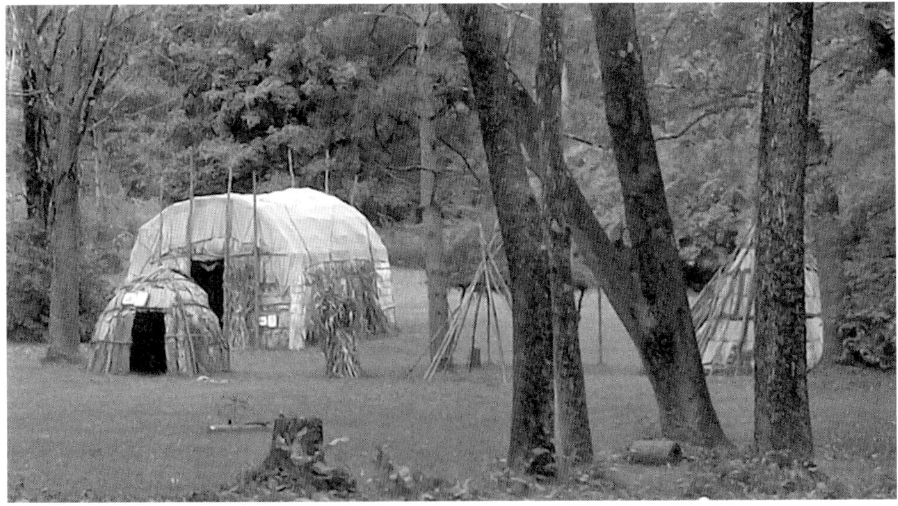

Reconstructed longhouse and wickiup (wigwam) at the Shawnee and Iroquois Peckuwe Village, George Rogers Clark Historic Park, Springfield, Ohio. *Courtesy of Carl A. Koehler.*

who was also tried in Canandaigua for the "high crime" of voting in the late 1800s. Anthony was found guilty and fined $100, which she did not pay. Also, in Canandaigua's debtors' prison, Jesse Hawley wrote his essays on the need to build the Erie Canal; these proved influential in moving the idea forward.

Today, most travelers pass through, perhaps staying at motels or getting a bite to eat along the main strip, without ever knowing these stories took place just a heartbeat away. Yet just outside Victor, New York, the Seneca nation has taken great strides to make sure its heritage is not lost. Here it has reconstructed a longhouse and the legacy of Ganondagan, once home to over one thousand natives. We are entrusted to learn the Senecas' story.

Legend of Bare Hill

Bare Hill rises above Canandaigua Lake by about five hundred feet. It was near this hill that a Seneca village once stood and here that they held council. No trees grow on Bare Hill. Seneca legend says this is because of a captured great snake.[*]

Once long ago, a boy found a very colorful snake. As boys will do, he caught it and took it home, but this was no ordinary snake. It had a voracious appetite, which the boy satisfied with insects and small creatures. As the snake grew, these did nothing to stave off its hunger, so the boy fed it larger animals.

The boy became a man and a hunter, and the snake grew, too. The young man needed to hunt for enough food for the snake, leaving little time for him to feed his family. People became afraid of the serpent, fearing it might not be satisfied with forest animals. It might eat one of them instead, and it did eat many. In fear, the people fled to a hilltop north of their village, all but a boy and girl who did not follow. The snake coiled itself around the village, crushing it to pieces. It did not see the boy and girl.

In a dream, Great Spirit told the little boy to shoot behind the snake's eyes. The next day, the very brave boy, being so small compared to the snake, shot his arrow between the scales of its head.

Mortally wounded yet strong, the snake writhed, thrashing its tail wildly across the nearby hill. The trees were crushed, laying the hill bare. The

*. Several sources were used to piece together the legend of Bare Hill, from a New York Times article to an individual's website and the Town of Canandaigua's website.

heads of people it had eaten scattered down the hillside as the serpent fell dead at last in the lake below. The hill has never again grown trees.

Stories of indigenous peoples are often tied to the landscape, and besides the legend of why the hill is bare, septaria stones found in the region are known to some as "Indian Heads."

Seneca elders once held an annual ceremony called *Genundowa*, or the "Festival of Lights," during which a council fire was made atop the hill. Fires were lighted throughout the valley as a sign of unity. Today, this ceremony is known as the Ring of Fire, taking place on the Saturday before Labor Day.

Bloomfield

East Bloomfield was settled in 1789 as part of the Phelps and Gorham Purchase, at the fringes of what had been the Seneca village of Gandougarae (destroyed by Denonville in 1687). This tiny village might be easily missed if not for its historic district, boasting forty-eight buildings of a historic nature, including homes, churches, an academy and others.

The village's founder, Deacon John Adams of Alford, Massachusetts, purchased the land on which the village sits. Additional pioneers followed the deacon, bringing Bloomfield's population to about sixty residents within one year. This is a good example of what a dynamic period it was. Once westward trails opened and land was made available, people flocked to these locations, even to the farthest reaches of the state's interior.

From its early days, Bloomfield was sustained by farming, with wheat being a major crop, and like other communities, it had its own flour mills, a distillery and a sawmill. As demand dictated, other industries grew along Mud Creek; these included a tannery, a gristmill, a cabinetmaker, a wool carder, blacksmiths, coopers, clock manufactories and a potash factory in the early 1800s. Bloomfield also produced the first natural gas pipeline around 1870. These pipelines were made of hollowed-out pine logs, and one ran twenty-five miles to Rochester. This is a remarkable variety of industries for a village with a population that is today under four thousand. Then again, this village lay along a major stagecoach line to Buffalo. It was also a crossroads for points north and south along Route 444.

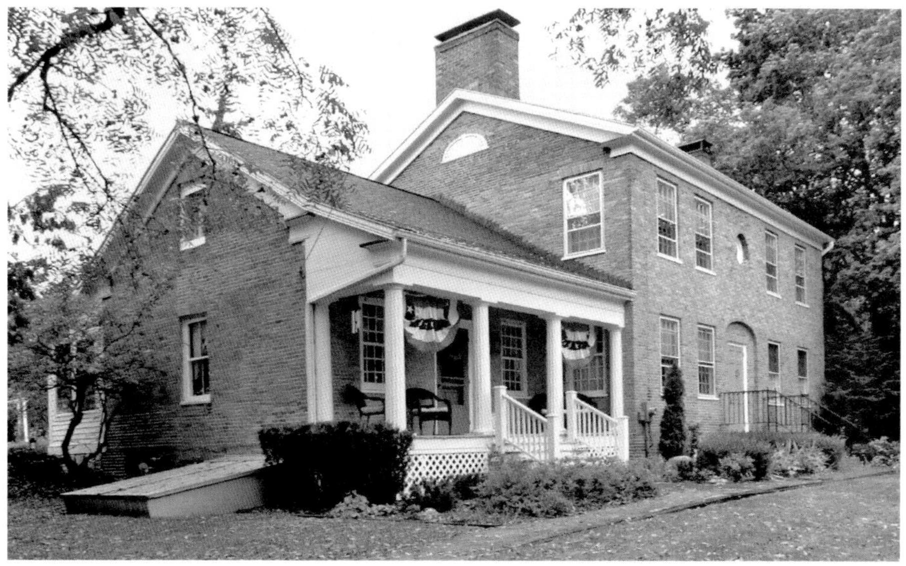

Abner Adams House. *Courtesy of the author.*

Two of Bloomfield's most esteemed citizens were Nathaniel Rochester, who went on to found the city of Rochester, north of Bloomfield, and Frederick Douglass, who lived there for a while.

Its claim to fame is the Northern Spy apple, first cultivated there in 1800 from a seedling imported from Connecticut. Sometimes referred to as Northern Pie apple, this fruit is considered one of the best for apple pies. Though not as popular today due to its irregularities and lack of disease resistance, for pie aficionados, the Northern Spy is still the one to beat.

Abner Adams was the eighth child of Bloomfield's founder. Born in 1772, long before his parents made the trek westward, his early years probably witnessed the colonies at war.

Many years later, after marrying Hannah Rowley, Abner purchased one hundred acres in Bloomfield from his brother-in-law. Then, in 1811, with a burgeoning family of six children, Abner bought an additional fifty-five acres and built a house, making a good living as a farmer. He also helped form a farm co-op, once located on Main Street in Bloomfield.

The Abner Adams House operates as a bed-and-breakfast today. Its bricks might have been made right in the village, as a brickworks was located there in the early 1800s. It is among Bloomfield's treasured architectures.

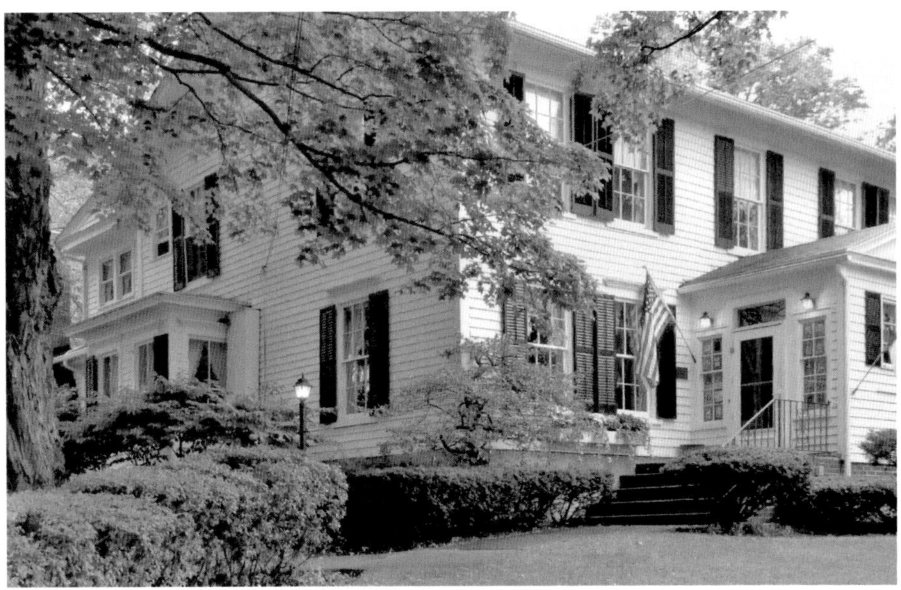

Holloway House. *Courtesy of the author.*

In 1835, Abner Adams moved his family closer to Rochester, where he became an engineer working with builders on the Erie Canal. The village where he settled is known today as Adam's Basin.

Even a tiny town can leave a lasting footprint and legacy. Other family members became renowned in their own right. Samuel Hopkins Adams, born in Dunkirk, New York, was the great-great-grandson of Bloomfield's founder, Deacon John Adams. He not only began the football program at Hamilton College but also wrote for the *New York Sun* and *McClure's* magazine. He was known for his investigative journalism, especially concerning health in the United States. Samuel wrote many novels, some of which may be viewed at the Abner Adams House.

Another of Bloomfield's renowned establishments is the Holloway House, located on Routes 5 and 20 proper. In 1808, a local blacksmith named Peter Holloway opened the former residence as a wayside tavern. By this time, there were many pioneers moving to settle in western New York and beyond, as well as military personnel on their way to Buffalo and Niagara Falls. Way stations like this were a necessity, and the Holloway Inn became a popular stop for many stagecoach lines.

During the Roaring Twenties and until 1928's stock market crash, the inn was operated by the Munson family as a restaurant for fine dining under the name Locust Lawn. It drew wealthier patrons from Buffalo and Rochester, whose chauffeurs proudly guarded their flashy automobiles. The name was later changed to Holloway House under new ownership in 1939. The elegant, earthy restaurant retains its colonial heritage today.

Destruction of Gandougarae

Gandougarae was a major Seneca village and the earliest Christian community in modern-day Genesee County. Jesuit missionary Jacque Fremin dedicated a chapel to Saint Michael there in 1668. Most residents of this village were captive Huron, giving it the nickname "town of captives."

Jacque Fremin, the same Jesuit who mentored Saint Kateri in the Mohawk Valley, visited what is now the region of Bloomfield, New York, during the Beaver Wars (1648–98). These wars were largely inter-tribal over hunting rights for beaver pelts, highly prized by Europeans. It was a tenuous era for the Jesuits and for the Indians, who had little knowledge of the white man's desire to rule this new world. When the boiling kettle overflowed, it spilled into the laps of the Indians, especially the Senecas.

The Marquis de Denonville arrived in Canada as governor of what was then called New France. His assignment in 1685 was to win Indian support. He viewed the powerful Iroquois Confederacy with its activities in the Beaver Wars as a nuisance, blocking the way to colonial profitability for his king, Louis XIV. As such, he set out to establish himself as a no-nonsense leader on France's behalf. In an act of blatant treachery, Denonville's forces captured fifty Iroquois sachems (chiefs) when they traveled to Montreal for talks. Denonville had them deported to France as slaves. This took place in 1687. The Iroquois validated Denonville's concern when over one thousand warriors brutally attacked the Lachine settlement near Montreal. Denonville's retaliation swept across western New York literally as fire, burning Seneca villages as he went, including the mission village of St. Michael, or Gandougarae.

In broad contrast, New York's colonial governor, Thomas Dongan, urged the Iroquois to declare war against France, making Dongan and his Indian allies enemies of Denonville. The stage for the coming French and Indian

War was being set on New York's frontier. Denonville went on from there to establish Fort Denonville in 1687 at the site of current-day Fort Niagara. All that remains of Gandougarae is a marker on Routes 5 and 20.*

Sonnenberg Gardens: Sunny Hill

Throughout our state's history, the affluent have owned "country" homes in upstate and central New York. So it was for Mr. and Mrs. Frederick Thompson.

Upon their marriage in 1863, banker Frederick Ferris Thompson and his new wife, the former Mary Clark, daughter of governor Myron Holley Clark, joined the ranks of New York City socialites. They purchased three hundred acres of farmland in Canandaigua for their summer home, keeping its name as Sonnenberg, meaning "Sunny Hill" in German. They continued to maintain their address in New York City as well. The glorious Canandaigua mansion was "just" their second home.

Over the following twenty years, the childless couple replaced the old farmhouse with the present-day forty-room mansion. Upon Frederick's death in 1899, Mary renovated the gardens as a living memorial to her beloved husband. Her design ideas were influenced by her travels to gardens worldwide, from medieval to Italianate to Japanese, both formal and informal.

When Mary died, her nephew Emory Clark inherited the estate. He then sold it to the federal government in 1931. Much of the farmland became a veterans' hospital. Its gardens suffered greatly at this time, leading to a public outcry in the mid-1960s. Finally, after a decade, Congress passed a bill establishing Sonnenberg Gardens as a not-for-profit. Restorations began in 1973.

It was almost an archaeological dig, as it was necessary to unbury old gardens and various structures such as fountains. The mansion itself had been divided up into various offices. These had to be carefully stripped away and the grandeur of a past age renewed using original blueprints and photographs. The public had never seen this playground for the wealthy until the bill was passed. Then, with crushing debts, the site was turned over for management by New York State in 2005.

---

*. The Catholic Encyclopedia is one of many sources used to research the Marquis de Denonville. As with all resources, it is important to remember the viewpoint of the source; in this case, a European Catholic perspective: http://www.newadvent.org/cathen/04732a.htm.

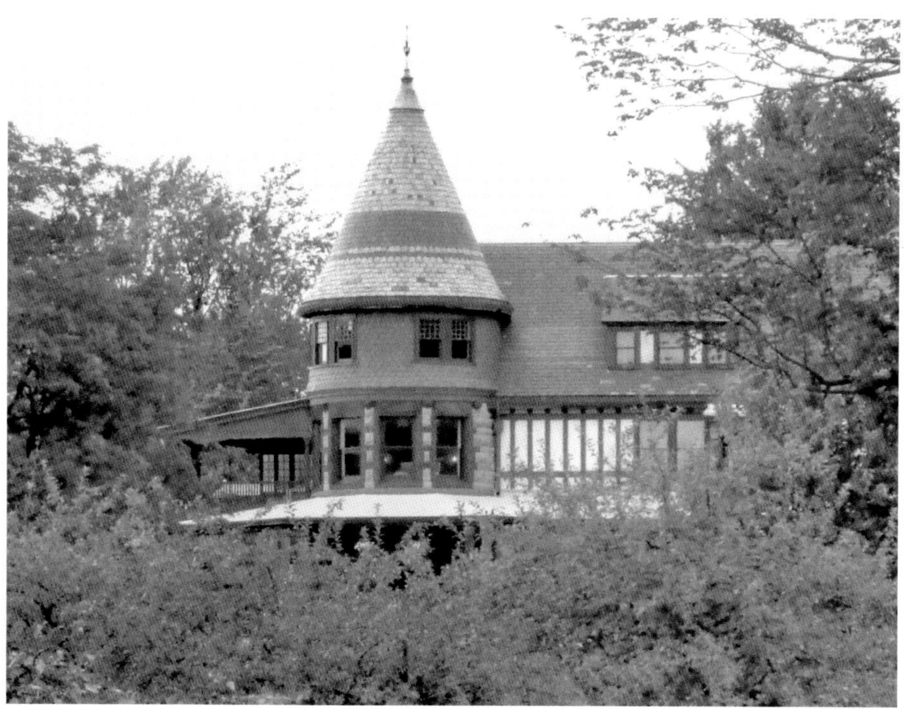

Sonnenberg Mansion tower. *Courtesy of the author.*

Sonnenberg is a glimpse of America's golden age of growth, industry and wealth and is among the most striking landscapes of that era. We are once again reminded that not only did war, water, hard work, courage and industry build the state, but it also required money to drive it forward.

VALLEY OF THE GENESEE

Defined by the Genesee River, this counterpart to the Mohawk Valley stretches from the Finger Lakes to the Niagara Frontier. Many Genesee Valley villages were settled as part of the Phelps and Gorham purchase, with officers of the Revolutionary War receiving the first lots. The farther west one travels, the later the settlements tend to be, as this was very much the wilderness interior until after the War of 1812. With few exceptions, settlements appear to radiate outward from Albany and Buffalo, coming together in this valley.

Lima: "The Crossroads of Western New York"

As with most of the Genesee region, Lima was once home to thousands of the Seneca people. Lima, founded by war veterans in 1788 as Charleston, underwent a name change in 1808 to avoid confusion with another Charleston, New York. Drawn to rich soil for farming, the population grew along with industries to serve it. Its location, many businesses and a seminary earned Lima the title "Crossroads of Western New York." Its many lovely homes were built to serve the seminary and its faculty.

Lima was home to Genesee Wesleyan Seminary (Genesee College), one of the first schools in the country to offer education to both men and women. The seminary opened its doors in 1822 but closed in 1870, when the

Methodist Church decided that Syracuse would be a better choice for the school's growth. Residents of Lima fought through the courts to maintain the school, thus sparing their economy. Nevertheless, New York State closed the academy for good in 1875. Many faculty and students relocated to Syracuse University.

The story of Lima mirrors that of many small towns along Routes 5 and 20. Changes in traffic patterns, growth of cities nearer to major waterways and loss of industry and institutions siphoned the population. When populations drop, so do their needs. Businesses follow suit, which affects the social and physical environments. Lima barely managed to hold its own, possibly with help from Eleanor Roosevelt's New Deal project, the National Youth Administration (NYA). The NYA moved into the former college, remaining until 1942. Today, Elim Bible Institute has revitalized the old campus.

Social life declines without people to pay for it. Playhouses, opera houses, schools and eventually many fine pieces of turn-of-the-century architecture deteriorate until they either collapse or are demolished. Many Americans have come to realize that building these structures today is cost prohibitive. The craftsmanship cannot be easily replicated. As such,

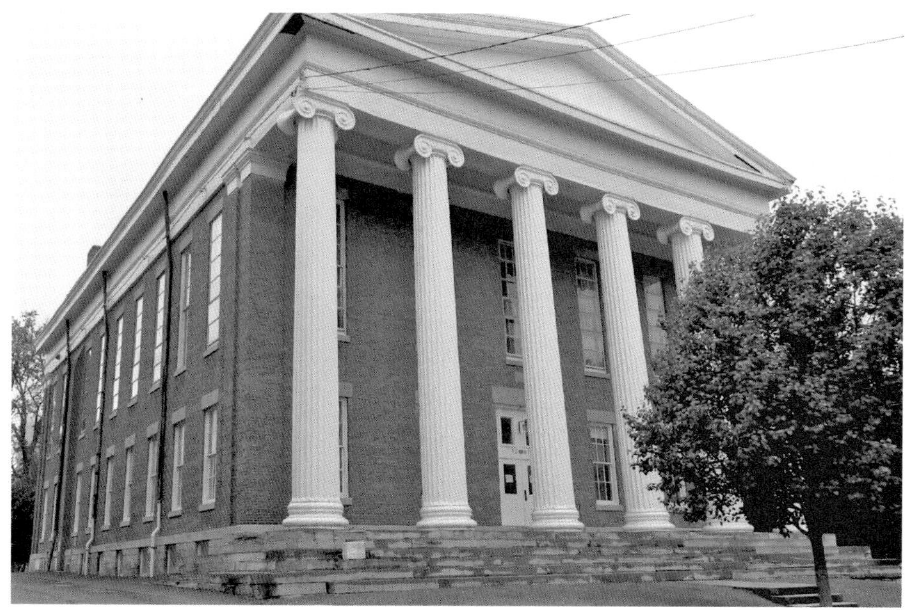

Elim Bible Institute. *Courtesy of the author.*

there has been a movement of restoration in many towns across the state, including Lima. There are fifty-eight structures in Lima that can be found on the New York State and National Registers of Historic Places.

Latter Rain Movement

Freedom to worship is a major foundation on which the country was built and part of the pioneering spirit across New York State. The Burned-Over District refers to a region of western New York that saw many nineteenth-century religious movements. This era was called the Second Great Awakening, when many utopian communities were built. Shakers, Spiritualists, Mormons and others sought freedom to explore their ideologies. Lima, at the edge of the Burned-Over District, experienced this fervor as the Latter Rain Movement in the mid-1900s.*

Latter Rain, a Pentecostal movement, did not begin in Lima, but the post–World War II revival from Sharon Orphanage in Saskatchewan, Canada, made its way to the western New York village, taking over the vacant college campus as Elim Bible Institute. "Elim" comes from the book of Exodus, meaning an "oasis in the wilderness."

Ivan Spencer, a farmer and Methodist minister, longed for spiritual fulfillment. He found it in 1924, when he and his wife, Minnie, opened Elim Bible Institute in Endwell, New York (near Binghamton). The school relocated several times before moving to Lima in 1951. While the Spencers did not begin the Latter Rain Movement, they did embrace it. Elim became a center for the movement in 1948.

Latter Rain's teaching of the Bible in stylized symbolic terms was criticized as heretical from the movement's beginnings. Because of this, the term "Latter Rain" is not widely used today.

Then, as now, Elim Institute's mission is "to prepare Spirit-filled Christian workers and servant-leaders for revival ministry worldwide."

*. There was no one defining source for the story about the Latter Rain Movement. Several were found online and pieced together. This is true of other movements found in this book, as well: Community Place, Ebenezer Community, Oneida Community and so on. Sources included town websites, individual pages, Wikipedia and others.

The American Hotel

The American Hotel is located at the crossroads in Lima. Although the building itself has changed, there has been a hotel at this location since 1790. Originally made of wood, the structure was replaced in 1840. Replaced once more in 1861 following two fires, the hotel has remained as it is seen today. It is one of Lima's architectural gems in its simplicity. Even the interior remains largely unchanged with a beautiful bar and an office counter from the Civil War period.

The Reynolds family has owned the three-story hotel since 1920. As is often the tradition, the family residence is located on the third floor. Second-floor rooms can still be rented, and a restaurant is found on the first floor.

During Prohibition years, the restaurant offered three meals a day to travelers. Being an inn, there is a bar that operated prior to the "dry" years.

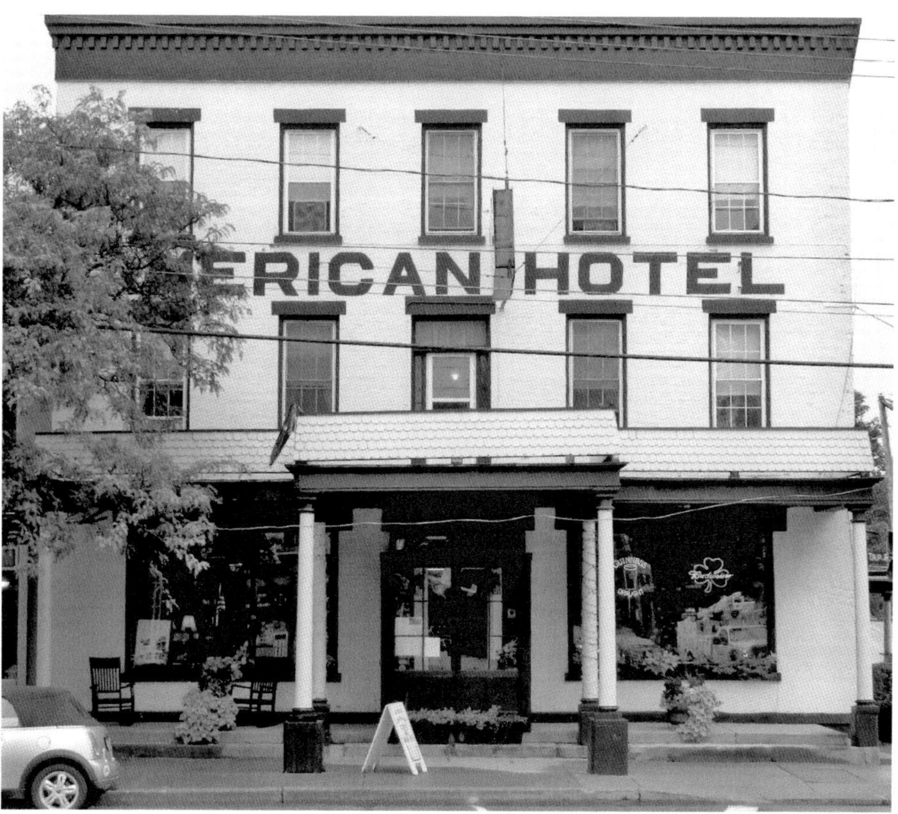

American Hotel, Lima. *Courtesy of the author.*

As with many establishments, including breweries of the era, the hotel converted it to a soda fountain. Following Prohibition, the hotel reverted to the sale of alcohol, making it the only such establishment in Lima at that time. No doubt, business was booming.

Typically, in the 1800s through the early 1900s, women were not served in taverns, or at least not at the bar itself. They had to be seated at a table and escorted by a male companion. Even the American Hotel's bar refused to serve women. However, the owners are proud to say that the sign stating, "No ladies served at the bar," hung by Grandfather Reynolds, was removed in 1955.

The hotel was well established by the time New York State built the Thruway and remained a viable business. This example of American architecture and entrepreneurship is still alive today—still in the Reynolds family and still serving up a helping of good ole family hospitality for travelers on Routes 5 and 20.

Avon, New York

Settled in 1785 as Hartford, Avon's name was changed in 1808 just like Lima's. The name comes from the River Avon in England. As a crossroads town, Avon was a stagecoach stop. When traveling east to west, Routes 5 and 20 separate here. Avon was once a Tuscarora village and the location of Genesee Valley's first flour mill, Ganson Mill. However, Avon's mainstay was its natural mineral springs.

Though it is sometimes called Avon Springs, the Senecas living here long before the town was formed called it Canawaugus, or "stinking waters." They meant only that it smelled of sulfur, not that it was poisoned in any way. These early natives valued its properties, bathing in and drinking from these springs. Today, Canawaugus is the name of a small community just west of Avon on Route 5.

Avon was as busy with its natural baths as was Saratoga Springs. During the 1800s, quite a few large hotels and inns were built to service pilgrims who journeyed to use the spas. These included the Livingston Inn (The Sanitarium), American Hotel (Congress Hall), the United States Hotel, the White Horse Tavern and Knickerbocker Hall.

Spas not only had bathhouses and rooms in which to stay, as well as dining for patrons, but they also offered other entertainments such as bowling alleys

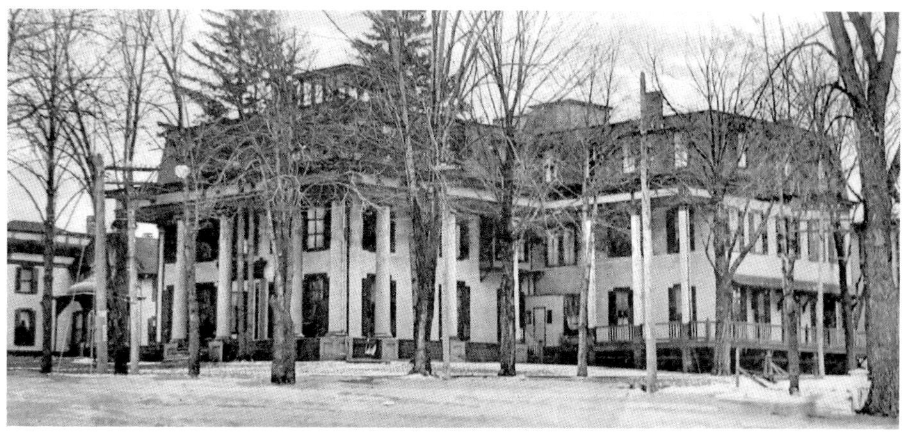

The Santarium, once the Livingston Inn. *Courtesy of the author.*

and beautiful gardens. In addition, Avon had a racetrack (Avon Springs Downs), something it needed to stay in competition with places like Saratoga Springs, which attracted wealthy patrons from New York City.

Today, Avon Springs is a park open to the community. The racetrack is still used by horse owners for training, and sulfur fumes do still occasionally bubble up as if to ask, "Do you remember?"

The Livingston Inn, built in 1866 and later renamed The Sanitarium, was reminiscent of those in the eastern part of New York State. No longer standing, this one-hundred-guest inn was moved to McPherson's Point in 1904 and destroyed by fire in the 1980s. Sadly, it was lost to us, as were other places of significance. The United States Hotel, taking up the entire block now housing the historical society and other offices, also went up in flames. A painting made by a resident sitting on his porch during the fire is on display at the museum.

Avon also had an establishment called the American Hotel, built in 1827, not to be confused with the one in Lima. The name was later changed to Congress Hall. Other towns had buildings named Congress Hall, too, such as Saratoga Springs and Lyons, New York. The American was a common name as well. An American Hotel is in use in Sharon Springs today. But few of these large old wooden hotels remain because they were prone to fire. Avon's Congress Hall burned in 1913.

Also gone is Knickerbocker Hall, a building erected by a physician named Devick Knickerbocker in the early 1820s. Knickerbocker Hall was on a hill between two sulfur springs. Dr. Knickerbocker was first in supporting the

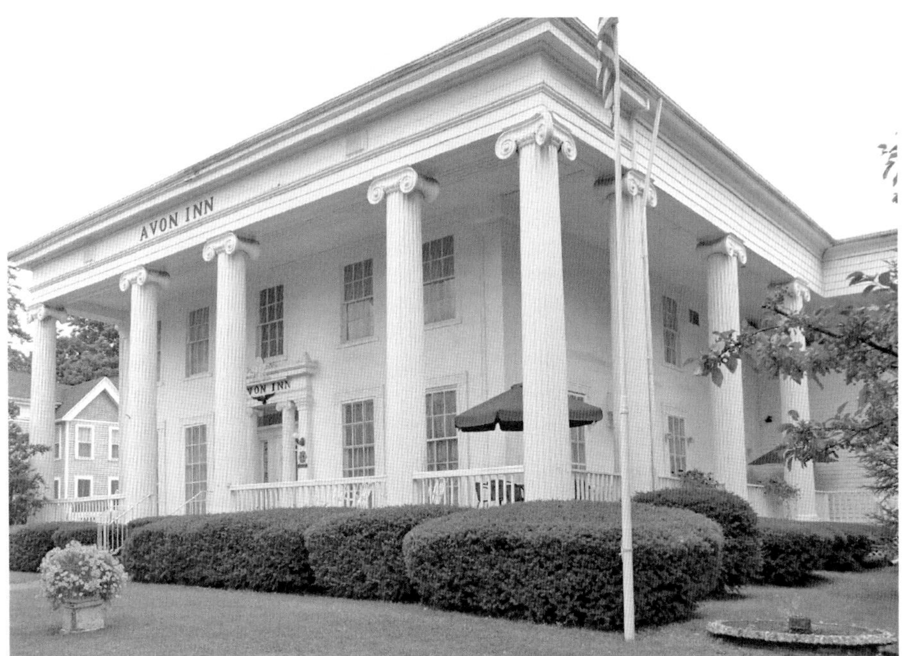

The Avon Inn. *Courtesy of the author.*

healing properties of mineral waters in Avon. His findings upon testing a wine glass of the water are fascinating. One spring was composed of sulfate of soda, carbonate and sulfate of lime, chloride of sodium and Epsom salts. The second spring included calcium in the mix. Even today, tired feet are soaked in Epsom salts.

Of all the hotels from Avon's spa era, only one really remains where visitors are welcome to stay and dine. Avon Inn was built in 1820. Today, there is also an old private residence owned by the Wadsworth family. Built in the mid-1800s by Asahel Wadsworth, although never a spa or tavern, the home is now operated as the White Oak Bed-and-Breakfast.

Additional sites worth noting are Avon's five-arch bridge, an 1850's railroad structure. One has to marvel at how these building projects were both well constructed and beautiful in their design details without the construction equipment we have today.

No longer there, Berry's Tavern, built by Gilbert R. Berry, Avon's first settler in 1789, served as a way station and trading post. Berry supplied another important service to pioneers: he ferried wagons across the Genesee River.

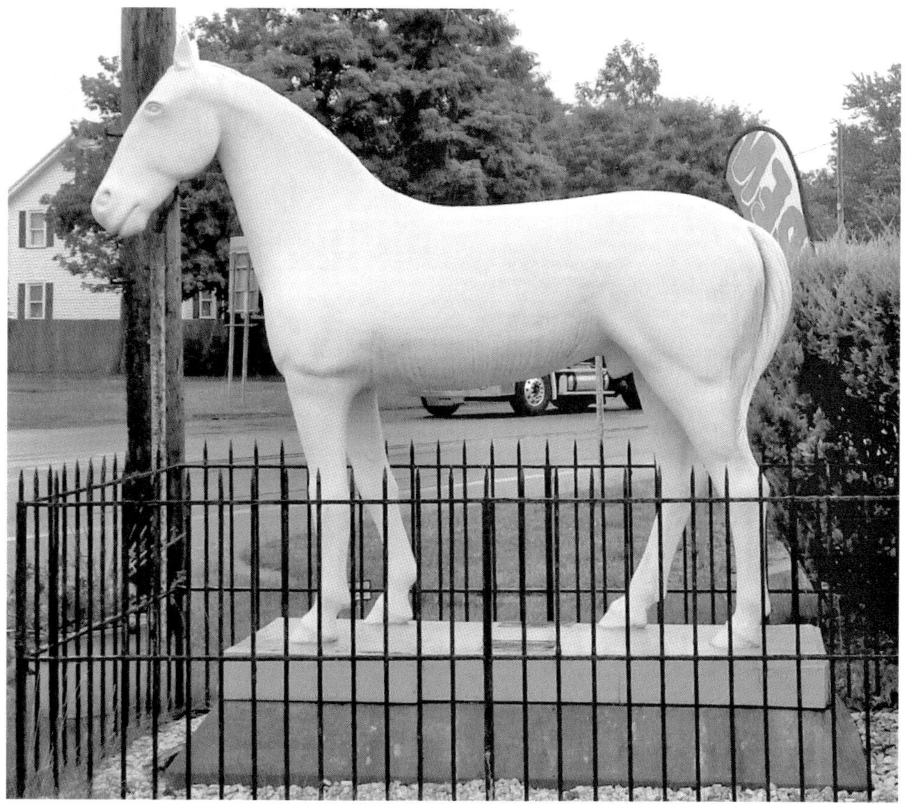

The White Horse Inn statue marker. *Courtesy of the author.*

One of the village's most lovely features is its circle green. Even in this day of bypasses and busy people, the road winds around the green, forcing travelers to take notice while recalling what small towns of our forefathers had to offer—communities with heart, a slower pace, a can-do spirit and a sense of adventure.

Avon also hosted a stagecoach station, again taken by fire in 1955. John Pierson (or Pearson) built the White Horse Tavern in 1812. Unlike the hotels of Avon, the tavern had no spa, yet it was a popular place to rest on the long journey to Buffalo or east toward Boston. A statue of a white horse was placed in front of the establishment in 1930. At the crossroads just east of town, travelers will see the white horse statue proudly marking the place where the tavern once stood.

Avon is truly a small town worth exploring for its architecture and charm, not to mention its good eating. Tom Wahls, although not a pioneer site, continues the pioneer spirit as a popular stop serving up great food to weary, hungry travelers since 1955. Avon has a modern-day manufacturer of note as well: it is in Avon that Cool Whip is made. Is it any wonder that another stop on the trail west has a Jell-O Museum?

Caledonia: Ganeodiya (Small Clear Lake)

Caledonia, settled in 1795 as South Hampton, is located on Route 5, approximately seven miles west of Avon, New York. The villages of York, Le Roy and Wheatland were all formed from the Caledonia tract. Its name is Roman for the Scottish Highlands and may honor Scottish settlers in the region. Indeed, many who fled Scotland seeking political and religious freedom came here.

As with Avon, Caledonia was known for its springs; in fact, several created a clear sweet lake rather than sulfurous mineral water. Big Springs, as it was called, emptied into Spring Creek and was alive with fish, namely trout. The Iroquois knew this pure lake as *Ganeodiya*. An ancient elm tree on its shore was their council place.

Throughout New York State's development, we have seen how water has acted as a guide for footpaths and as transportation. These waters have quenched thirst or cleansed and healed the body. They have offered entertainment, and they have powered industry. Big Springs also offered a meeting place, not only for native councils but for those fleeing the South following the Civil War as well. When Reconstruction as a whole failed to bring the ailing South back to some sense of normalcy, Reverend Clayton Coles, a Confederate soldier and servant to General Stonewall Jackson, arrived with many former slaves, establishing Mumford Second Baptist Church on the bank of Big Springs. The reverend was caretaker of Wheatland Baptist Cemetery, where he now resides eternally.

Caledonia highlights another aspect of our waters: sustainability of aquatic life. In 1864, Seth Green of Rochester used these crystal waters for his experiments in fish propagation. As a result, Green started a fish hatchery in Caledonia. Today, it annually releases 800,000 trout in New York State lakes and streams, proving once more how water created New York State and continues to sustain its communities.

Nearby is Genesee Country Village, a museum village of homes and businesses from throughout upstate New York. Here one will find the homestead of Caledonia's John MacKay, a spirited entrepreneur. His former land is now a wildlife preserve.

Pavilion's Gratwick Estate

Somewhat off the beaten trail of Route 20 is the sleepy little town of Pavilion. It was here in the 1900s, during the arts and crafts movement, that William Gratwick built his country estate, today known as Linwood Gardens. Gratwick also had a home in Buffalo; sadly, it has been demolished.

As with Geneva, New York, known for its nursery period, Gratwick Estate was where William bred American peonies. Arthur Saunders, his employer, began this work. American peonies are today considered among the most beautiful in the world.

The gardens are open to the public each spring for the Tree Peony Festival of Flowers and during other special events. It is a private residence.

Le Roy: Birthplace of Jell-O

Le Roy is located just fourteen miles west of Avon on Route 5. There seem to be many instances of name changes in the Genesee Valley, and Le Roy is no exception. Founded in 1812 as Bellona, the name became Le Roy in 1813 in honor of Herman Le Roy, an original landowner of what was called the Triangle Tract. Even though its official founding was late, its first settlement was in 1793, and its first established business was a tavern.

Oatka Creek powered the usual pioneer industries. Later industries were unique, including the manufacture of patent medicines and household chemicals such as mustard plaster and rat poison. In addition, Le Roy produced brooms, wagons and other goods. However, Le Roy's number one commodity was salt from several salt wells within its boundaries. Three railroads passing through the village helped transport these products, increasing its economy. With so much railroad traffic, wares needed to be stored safely. Le Roy had what was considered by some to be one of the world's largest cold storage warehouses. There was also a grain elevator and three large malt houses. However, these were not Le Roy's only claims to fame. A medicinal experiment became "America's favorite dessert."

Using gelatin dates to the early Egyptians, and many Victorians loved it for creating gelled dishes. Gelatin was first patented in England in 1754 as a wood glue. Nearly one hundred years later, in 1845, Peter Cooper received a patent for the first powdered gelatin mixture. With the availability of household refrigeration, all that remained was for someone to recognize gelatin as a food substance rather than a substance used to gel other foods. That task fell on a resident carpenter named Pearle Wait.

Many people made their own remedies for any number of ills. These were typically created from herbs as salves, tinctures or teas. Pearle Wait was making cough medicine and laxative tea in 1897, perhaps using gelatin as a means of preserving his concoctions in solid form. Wait inadvertently created a fruity dessert his wife named Jell-O.

Without money to market his discovery, Wait sold the rights in 1899 to a school dropout who was already manufacturing medicines in Le Roy, including the medicated egg that killed lice on egg-laying chickens. That young man, who purchased the formula for $450, a fair sum then, was Orator Frank Woodward. Sales in two years amounted to over $200,000. Woodward died in 1906 at age forty-nine without the opportunity to fully experience his success.

Almost as interesting as the product is the pioneering method with which Jell-O was sold. Do you remember when Fuller Brush salesmen, Avon ladies and vacuum salesmen came to your door? Jell-O might have been the product that started it all. In fact, Jell-O's marketing technique is what made it so successful. Woodward sent salesmen in wagons sporting signage about Jell-O out to the streets and into the countryside. They made sure their rigs were seen at fairs and other social gatherings, outside churches and at parties. There was a print campaign also, with posters, handbills, billboards and magazine ads featuring the product's mascot, four-year-old Elizabeth King, the "Jell-O Girl." It didn't take long for this campaign to spread across America, giving Le Roy a lasting, tasty legacy.

Although Jell-O is no longer manufactured in Le Roy, there is always the Jell-O Museum, not to mention, "Always room for dessert."

Stafford

The small settlement of Stafford had a big beginning. It was the first settlement in the Holland Land Tract, making it Genesee County's oldest settlement. Founded in 1798, when surveyor Joseph Ellicott selected it as the eastern border of the tract, it has never been without a resident. The historic district consists of two private homes, a church, a seminary, a store, an Odd Fellows Hall and a memorial park. One of the two homes was built in 1809 and is the oldest in Genesee County.

The Bethanys

Bethany is about twenty-one miles west of Avon at the crossroads for Batavia. The town is made up of Bethany Center, East Bethany and West Bethany. Founded in 1803, it was once part of Batavia. Very rural, Bethany remained fairly small and of little consequence as pioneer settlements go. However, it does have a fascinating history.

Bethany Center was the first settlement within town borders. It had shops and other businesses, as well as an academy. Because not every village had a school and settlements were distant on poor roads, students sent to Bethany Academy were housed with local families during their educations.

Tonawanda and Little Tonawanda Creeks converge in West Bethany, allowing it to supply water power for small industry. One of these mills was a cloth mill still in business until the late 1900s.

East Bethany was the second settlement in the town, with additional shops and businesses, and it tells the most interesting story. It was home to the county poorhouse.

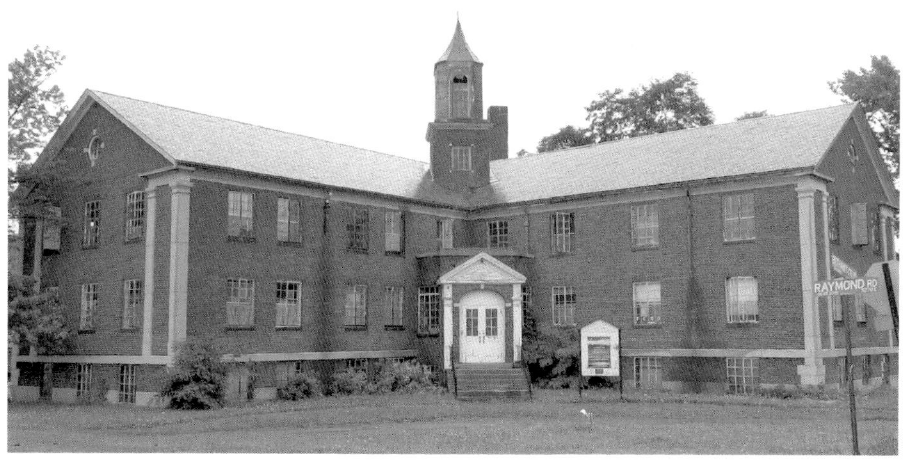

Rolling Hills Asylum. *Courtesy of the author.*

Rolling Hills Asylum, as it is called today, was Genesee County's poor farm. Many such places existed in the 1800s. Even Canandaigua had its debtors' prison. It was common practice as a means of social services to throw debtors and the homeless into communal facilities such as poorhouses. These institutions might include orphans, the elderly and the mentally and physically disabled. Even criminals and the insane were sometimes mixed in. In short, those we now place in prisons, rehab, public housing, shelters, retirement homes and hospitals were all housed in the same place, though separated into different buildings or wings according to their needs. It was the stuff of Charles Dickens novels, but this was not someplace in Europe.

Genesee County Home was formed in 1826. Its initial building was a tavern at the intersection of Bethany Center and Raymond Roads. It received its first residents in January 1827. Even those deemed insane were put there until 1887, when it was decided they should go elsewhere.

The county home was a self-sufficient working farm of over two hundred acres. A forest on the property supplied heating fuel. All able-bodied inmates (residents) were expected to work the farm. Livestock and crops were raised for food. There was also a bakery. In addition, they crafted items for sale to help fund the institution. Local morticians purchased coffins made there, and of course, some were needed for the home itself.

Supposedly, the facility had its own cemetery for those who could not afford burial elsewhere. Even though many deaths were recorded over its 147-year history, no record of these pauper burials has been found. The cemetery, if it existed, is unrecognizable. However, in 2004, five headstones were found in the basement of one of the buildings and might have been from this burial ground.

The facility served other purposes before finally closing its doors in 1974. It was the Genesee County Infirmary, caring for a variety of illnesses, tuberculosis among them, and the Genesee County Nursing Home.

A memorial and the five headstones now stand in Genesee County Park, which covers the bulk of the two hundred acres. Wooden structures such as dorms were torn down, leaving only a brick building, barn and carriage house. Ten years of abandonment have taken their toll. Today, its fourth private owner holds ghost hunts by appointment at Rolling Hills Asylum.

It is important to consider that although we might not appreciate how the residents of the Genesee County Home were treated, when we ask what sustains a community, we must remember that these institutions employed many local citizens. Once the poor farm closed, locals became unemployed and often moved someplace else.

BATAVIA AND BEYOND

Darien and Darien Center: Osoontogeh (Place of the Turkeys)

Continuing west from Bethany, travelers pass through the town of Alexander and near its village, said to have the largest cobblestone structure used for education in North America and the only cobblestone town hall. A few more miles west is Darien Center, in lands once occupied by the Senecas. Darien, once named South Pembroke, is best known for nearby Darien Lake Theme Park.

This rural community was settled in 1803. Orange Carter, from Vermont, was its first permanent settler in 1805. Carter assisted in local land surveys, perhaps working with the Holland Land Company in Batavia and receiving his land as payment, as did many surveyors. He was a volunteer in the War of 1812. Carter's brother arrived in 1806, followed by more and more settlers, opening inns, mills and other businesses. Before the town hall was built, town meetings were held in the local tavern. Many roads were not paved, even as late as 1911. Farming was Darien's main industry, supplying food to many nearby cities, including Buffalo, the second-largest city in the state.

Two streams and their offshoots web the town, supplying water for industry. One is Eleven Mile Creek, and the other is Murder Creek, the latter giving rise to at least two local legends.*

*. The legend of Murder Creek is taken from a handful of sources, including the following Erie County source. Since no actual Native American story or historical reference could be found to back up the first legend, we must assume it is a local fiction. The story of Sadie McMullen is well-known: http://www2.erie.gov/parks/index.php?q=legend-murder-creek.

Legend of Murder Creek

Murder Creek runs between Darien on Route 20 and Akron, New York, on Route 5, both cited for how Murder Creek got its name. A naming story involving Native Americans takes place in about 1820. A second story takes place in 1890 and is frighteningly true.

Several campy renditions of the naming story can be found, all intended to be sensational. These variations have a handful of elements in common. They all agree that there was a young native woman and at least one suitor, as well as a local pioneer family who helped the young woman. Nobody can say for certain whether any version is factual. People, then as now, have a curiosity about their origins, and stories have always been used to explain the whys and wherefores.

The legend of Murder Creek says that a man named John Dolph purchased land in Darien (or Akron). Dolph was either alone in the midst of building a sawmill near Murder Creek or inside his cabin with his family when a cry for help was heard. Upon opening the door, Dolph found a very distressed young Indian woman who hurriedly explained that a white man named Sanders had killed her family and was threatening to take her away. One story says Sanders wanted her for his wife; the other says he wanted her as a captive.

The tale continues by claiming that Dolph chased Sanders off, saying he had not seen an Indian woman. Sanders watched the house and determined she was indeed within. When Dolph was away, leaving his wife alone with the young woman, Sanders tried to take her. The native woman had a sweetheart, who just happened to be there to rescue his beloved. A struggle ensued. Weapons were drawn. Blood was spilled into the creek. First, Sanders went down under the tomahawk, and then the native fell from his wounds. Dolph, some distance away, heard the young woman's death chants and found her cradling her lover. Young lovers who walk the creek bed might hear her cry. Is it a warning? An echo? Either way, one truth exists: Murder Creek attracted death in 1890.

Seventeen-year-old Sadie (Sarah) McMullen sometimes looked after six-year-old Delia Brown and was the Browns' housekeeper. Eight-year-old Nellie May Connor had come to play with Delia. At about eight o'clock in the evening of November 1, 1890, Sadie asked to take the little girls to the local store on an errand. As they walked, Sadie lured them onto a railroad trestle, fifty feet over Murder Creek near Akron, New York. Once in the center of the bridge, Sadie grasped eight-year-old Nellie May Connor and pushed her off the bridge. She then turned on screaming six-year-old Delia Brown, tossing her over like a rag doll.

Sadie threw herself into the water at a much lower height. Her cries for help alerted rescuers, who found her floundering. Rescuers tugged Sadie from the water as she screamed uncontrollably for them to let her go back in. Sadie was carried to the Browns' home, and as they were tending her, the family began to ask questions about the children's whereabouts. Sadie chillingly replied, "What children? Were they with me?"

Frantically, a search party scoured the creek banks. Finally, at 3:00 a.m., they recovered Nellie's broken body. A short time later, they found little Delia alive but with debilitating injuries. Court testimony stated that upon being lifted to safety, little Delia's first coherent words were shocking: "Sarah was smart to throw us off of the bridge."

Later, eleven-year-old Dan Flynn also gave testimony that he saw Sadie pulling the girls toward the bridge that night. There was no shortage of testimony against Sadie McMullen, and during the trial, disturbing evidence of Sadie's troubled childhood came forward. Nonetheless, the trial of Sadie McMullen was short, lasting just two days in March 1891.

The electric chair had been invented a year prior, and everyone wondered, "Would the state electrocute its first woman?" Instead, the jury found Sadie innocent by reason of insanity. She was sent to Buffalo State Hospital (an asylum), where she remained until August 19, 1893. The hospital's superintendent declared Sadie perfectly sane, and she was released. As of today, nobody knows what became of Sadie McMullen after her release. One can only hope the superintendent was right.

Batavia

Batavia was home to the Holland Land Company, which is a museum today. The city derives its name from a region in the Netherlands. Batavia is the seat of Genesee County, once including all lands from the Genesee Valley up to Niagara Falls and the Pennsylvania state line.

It was from Batavia that many surveyors, including its founder, Joseph Ellicott, set off into the western New York wilderness to carve the communities as they are today. From the easternmost border of Stafford to Buffalo, the western frontier became settled. Pioneers who did not set down roots traveled to the Ohio Valley and beyond from this point.

Batavia is where early settlers filed their deeds, many stocking up on supplies before arriving at newly purchased land on the Niagara frontier. This tract of land, over three million acres, was purchased from Phelps and Gorham between 1792 and 1793.

Joseph Ellicott, who laid out Buffalo, founded the village of Batavia in 1802 and established the land office. However, the land purchase required its former owner, Robert Morris, to make good with the Iroquois before the land could be settled. A meeting to do so was held at Geneseo, once called Big Tree for the large oak located near the river. Three thousand natives were present, including Chief Red Jacket, who vehemently opposed the sale. However, the final decision was up to the women of the nation, as was customary among the Iroquois. Having been "bribed" with trade goods, the women agreed to the sale. The chiefs signed the Treaty of Big Tree. Geneva's Horatio Jones, who interpreted at the signing of the Treaty of Canandaigua, also interpreted for this event.

As county seat and home to the land office, Batavia was poised to be a great city, but in 1825, developers of the Erie Canal bypassed it in favor of a more northerly route, taking the canal and its business to Rochester and Buffalo. Once land settlements were depleted, Batavia then turned to small industry and agriculture.

Pembroke: Oageh (On the Road)

Named for Pembroke in Wales, this small village settled by David Goss in 1804 was once part of Batavia. David Goss turned his home into the town's first public house, Old White Tavern.

The town was divided into villages and hamlets with other fascinating names such as East Pembroke, originally named Ellicott Mills for Joseph Ellicott. Today's Pembroke was Richville after businessman Charles Rich. Pembroke Center was called Frog Hollow. Also within town borders was a portion of the Tonawanda Indian Reservation, once a larger Iroquois village at current-day Indian Falls.

Its most famous resident was Seneca chief and "Keeper of the Western Door" Ely Parker, born in 1828 on the Tonawanda reservation in a cabin overlooking Indian Falls. Ely Parker was General Grant's secretary during the Civil War. He was the first native commissioner of Indian affairs and is buried at the statue of Red Jacket in Forest Lawn Cemetery in Buffalo, New York.

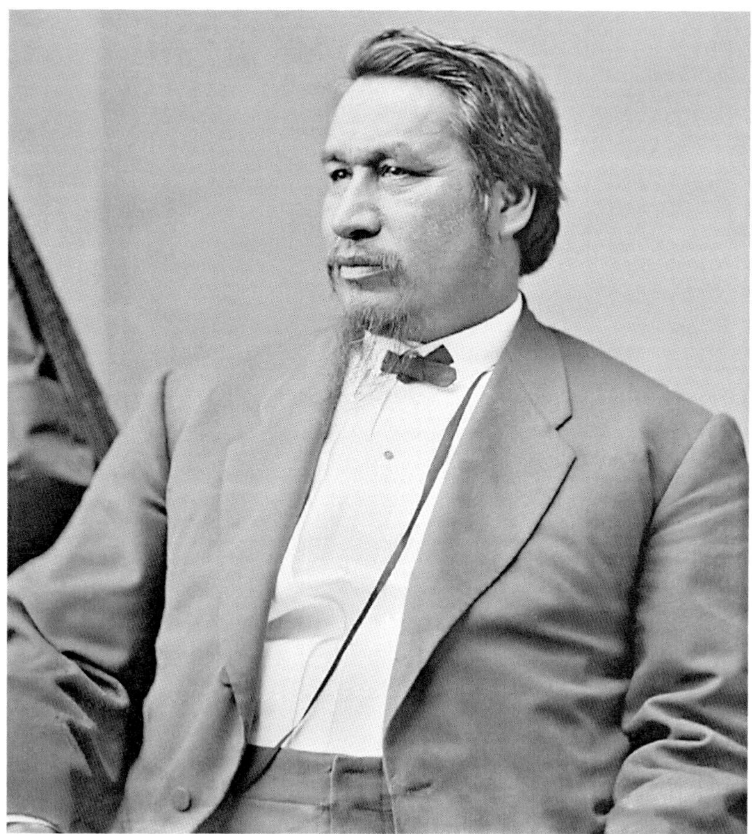

Colonel Ely S. Parker, circa 1860–circa 1865. *Courtesy of the U.S. National Archives and Records Administration, Photographs and Other Graphic Materials.*

Pembroke's main business has been farming, but nearby major roadways and its proximity to Buffalo and Rochester make it a "bedroom" community today.

Alden

Alden was settled by Moses Fenno in 1810 and named for an earlier resident. There were twelve people forming the village by 1811. The creeks were perfect for mills, and soon the village began to populate. The town also comprises the villages of West Alden, Alden Center, Crittenden, Peter's

Corners, Mill Grove, Town Line and Wende. Many old, charming homes can still be found.

Even though the village grew quickly in a short time, it nearly became a ghost town during the War of 1812. Refugees from Buffalo, which was burned by the British, warned outlying villages, and they, too, emptied. However, many returned after the war, resettling in 1814. The first school appeared one year later, along with one of the pioneers' most common early businesses—a tavern. The town filled with prosperous citizens. In the mid- to late 1800s, many German immigrants inhabited Alden after fleeing troubles in their homeland. In addition, three railroad lines contributed to growth.

In 1854, residents built a seminary. By 1875, the village had a couple of hotels and its own newspaper. Alden also had Spring Cheese factory and a natural gas company, with natural gas being found throughout western New York.

Railroads and mills do not an economy make, though they help. The 1891 discovery of a reservoir of natural black water placed Alden in the forefront. This mineral water was uncovered while men were drilling for natural gas. People came from all across the state and beyond to partake of the healing waters at Black Water Baths, especially European immigrants who knew the value of such baths, common in their homelands.

A New York State commission investigated mineral baths in 1936, finding Black Water's minerals effective for treating joint ailments such as arthritis and rheumatism, as well as blood pressure and skin diseases.

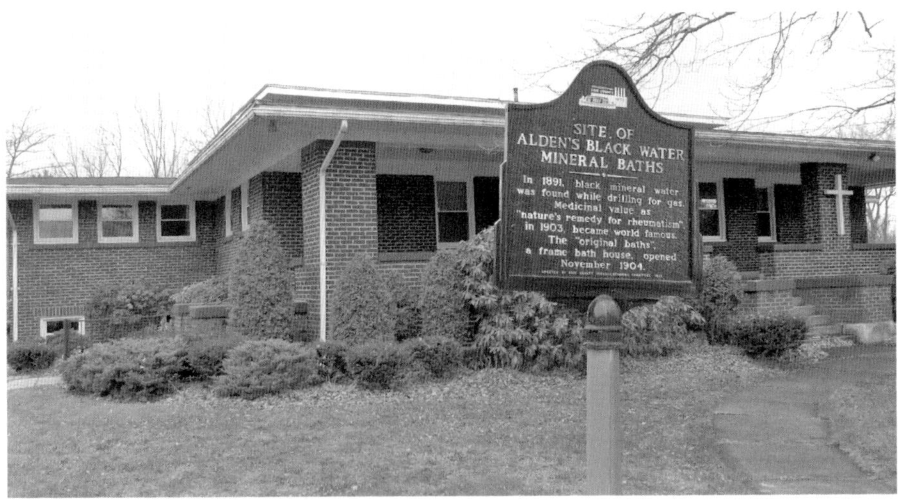

The last remaining building of the Black Water spa, now used by a church for services. *Courtesy of the author.*

Additional bathhouses, inns and boardinghouses opened to handle an overflow of patrons coming to the small town. Black Water Baths were open from 1904 until 1964. Fires destroyed most structures associated with the baths, but one does remain. St. Aidan's Episcopal Church on West Main Street currently operates from this last building.

Town Line: Last Confederate Holdout

The year was 1861, and the country, not yet one hundred years old, was at war again. Disagreements over states' rights divided the nation, and the Southern states voted to secede. They created their own constitution and elected their own president. An invisible line was "drawn in the sand." The Mason-Dixon line, still representing the division that could have destroyed the country in its infancy, did not stop the spread of dissent. Even Northern households found themselves torn as some family members sided with the South. Then there was the hamlet of Town Line, New York, on Route 20.

Very much rooted in the North, located between Alden and Lancaster, New York, this small community voted eighty to forty-five to secede from the nation. It really did! Some residents even joined the Southern army, though many did fight for the Union. The Federal government largely ignored this act of treachery. No actions were taken against the town. Some residents of Town Line once proudly referred to their community as the last holdout of the Confederacy, and some even thought of themselves as natural-born Confederates.

Town Line rejoined the Union after pressure following the end of World War II. Patriotism spread like wildfire when soldiers returned home. Many Confederate communities reconciled, but it was not Town Line's plan to rejoin the Union, even though it received many letters begging it to do so. It was only after a very "insistent plea" from President Harry Truman that it finally acquiesced. A ceremony was held with great fanfare. Film crews were present as the Confederate flag was finally lowered on that day in 1946 in western New York. However, it was not until decades later that the town's fire company voted to remove the Confederate patch from its uniform. Town Line truly was the "Last Confederate Holdout," at least in the North. To this day, nobody recalls why Town Line seceded.

Clarence: Tanumnogao (Place of Hickory Bark)

As with many western New York towns, Clarence was divided into small villages. As Erie County's first town, founded in 1808, Clarence gets its name from England's House of Clarence.

One of the town's first settlers was Asa Ransom, a silversmith from Geneva, New York. Ransom arrived in 1799. A Revolutionary War officer, he established a tavern in his home. Besides affording a place for pioneers to stay as they traveled to their new land, it was sometimes part of the deal made with land agents. A pioneer who purchased land and built a tavern might be given a very good deal on the land. Ellicott sold to Ransom for a meager two dollars per acre with no long-term interest. Tavern lots were often several miles apart, about what the average settler could travel in a day.

Not only did Ransom run the tavern, but he also built a sawmill and a gristmill. His name graces several locations in western New York, including Ransom Road and Ransomville. Joseph Ellicott opened a Holland Land office in Ransom's tavern, which certainly drew residents. Some also speculate that Ellicott boarded at the Ransom home. Travelers and locals still enjoy evenings at the Asa Ransom House.

Few, if any, additional settlers arrived in Clarence until 1801. Born in 1801, Asa Ransom Jr. was the first child born in Clarence Hollow, as the village became known.

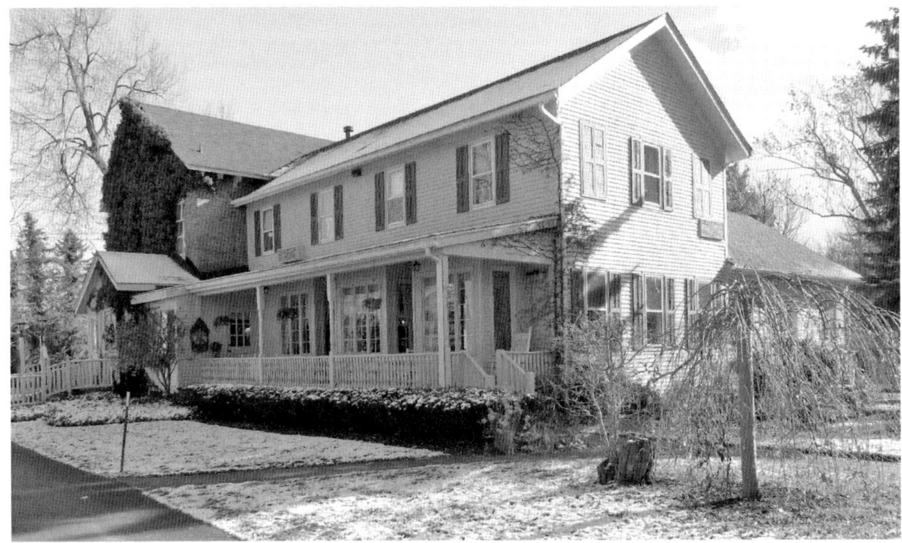

Asa Ransom House. *Courtesy of the author.*

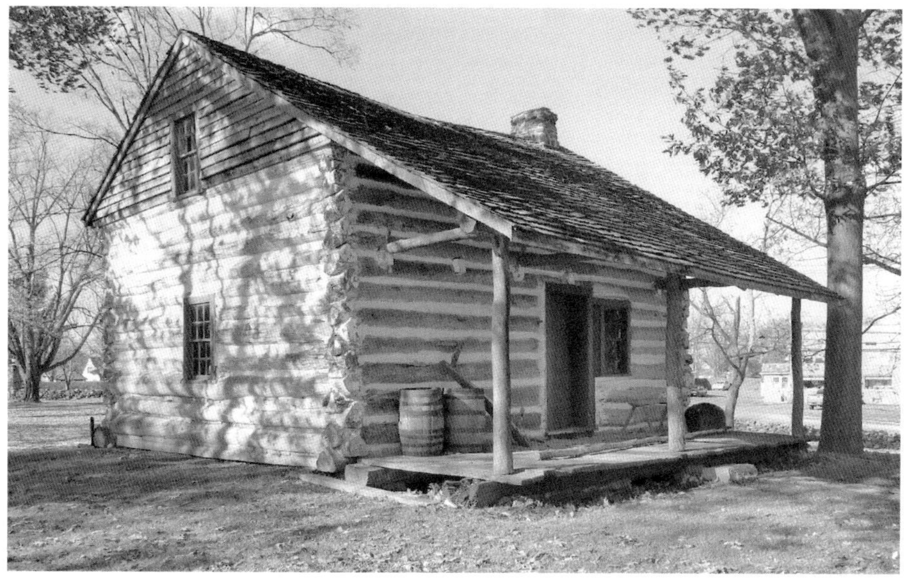

A typical log home, Clarence Historical Museum. *Courtesy of the author.*

The Industrial Revolution came to Clarence. Industries were mostly mining for potash and gypsum.

Many lovely historic homes line the main streets within Clarence's borders, from Clarence Hollow to Clarence Center. The Clarence Historical Society Museum at the edge of Clarence Town Park includes an example of a very early log cabin.

It would be remiss to forget Clarence's great tragedy, even though it was modern. On February 12, 2009, Colgan Air Flight 3407 crashed into a home in Clarence Center's peaceful village, killing everyone on board as well as a resident of the home. Not only was it a local tragedy, but it was also a national one. A memorial to this loss is found there today.

Harris Hill

Harris Hill, a hamlet of Clarence, is located about five miles west of Clarence Hollow. Its founder was Asa Harris, also an officer in the Revolutionary War. As with Asa Ransom, Harris's land purchase led to a tavern being built. The tavern was at the top of a low hill, thus Harris Hill.

Harris Hill has a long-standing tradition of helping those in need. During the War of 1812, when the British burned Buffalo, many refugees from the city fled to Harris Hill. Even the *Buffalo Gazette*'s printing presses found refuge there. Following the war, when citizens returned to the city, Harris Hill reverted to a small, quiet community. Harris's tavern, a stagecoach stop, was also a station for the Underground Railroad. A basement cave allowed freed slaves to escape beneath the road into nearby wet forestlands. The tavern stood at the site of a historical marker on Route 5. The cave beneath the business on that site has long since been filled for reasons of safety.

Lancaster/Depew

Once inhabited by mammoth hunters and later by the Senecas, Lancaster, New York, was part of the Holland Land Purchase. Early records show Alanson Eggleston to have purchased the first land in 1803. To put into perspective how remote these hamlets and towns were at the time, a road was not cut from Buffalo to Lancaster until 1808. Even then, it would have been a narrow dirt road, subject to ruts and reclamation by the forests.

Other pioneers trickled into the town, building the necessary mills and small businesses—and, of course, a tavern—around which the village was formed. There are a handful of villages in the township. The village of Lancaster is the most significant. Around 1830, many Germans settled here, as they did in Clarence and other nearby locations.

The first schoolhouse was built in 1810, showing that a small population of children was present at that time. An academy was built in 1843. For a short time, there was the Oakwood Institute, an agricultural college, but it was unsuccessful. In 1849, several wealthy Dutchmen settled in the village, building many lovely homes and supporting local businesses.

One of the industries unique among the communities of Routes 5 and 20 was Lancaster Glassworks. It employed eight glassblowers from Pittsburg. Following the glassworks were two tanneries, one that became a soap factory, an iron foundry, a brick factory, a malt house and a sawmill. Three fires in 1894 and another in 1896 burned most of these buildings. A manufacturer of church organs and a hotel were also established. A while later, a local entrepreneur attempted to drill for petroleum. This proved fruitless, but Lancaster remained a booming community. As such, Lancaster had a literary society and remains proud of its opera house. Typical of opera houses of the

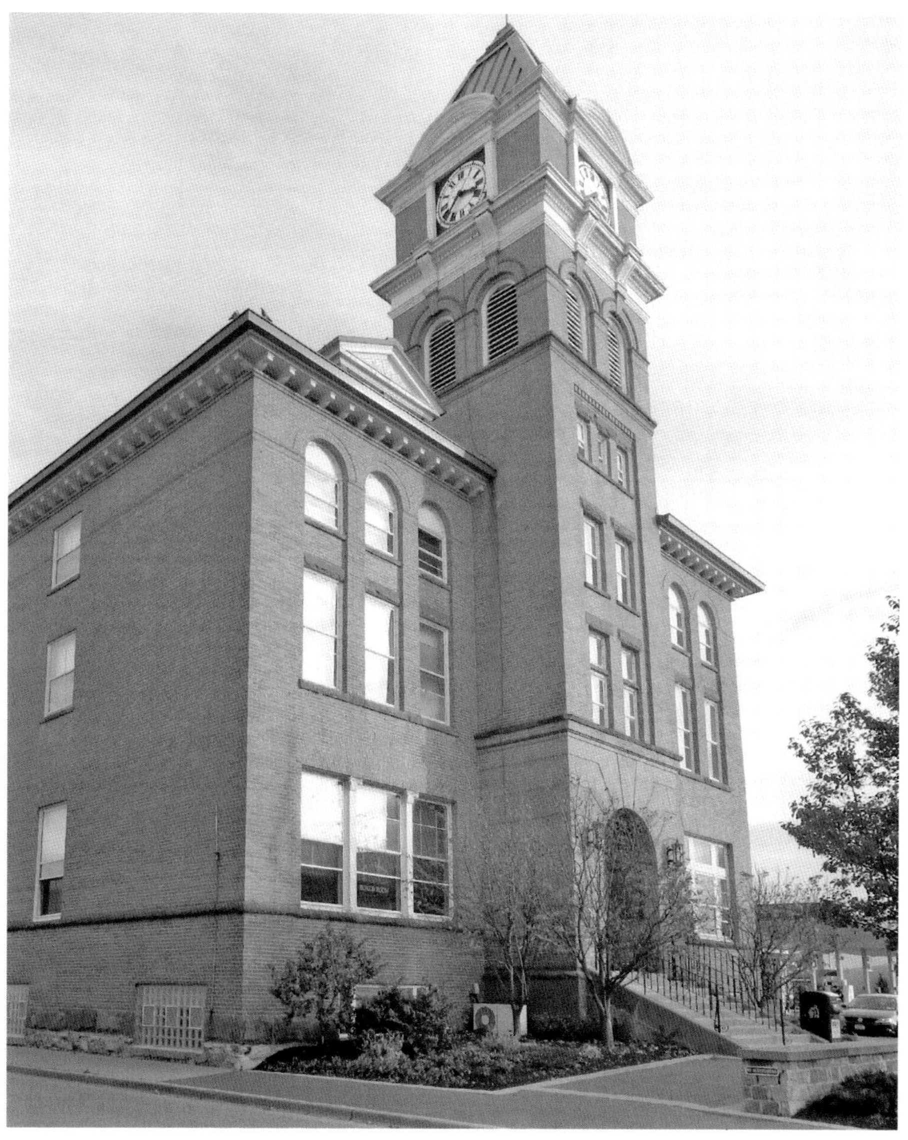

Lancaster Opera House. *Courtesy of the author.*

period, Lancaster Opera House served as a government building, meeting place and a music hall. It was used during World War II for sewing and packing parachutes.

Perhaps one of Lancaster's most prominent citizens was Dorothy Thompson, born in 1893. *Time* magazine recognized her in 1939 as one of

America's most influential women, next to Eleanor Roosevelt. A journalist and radio broadcaster, Thompson was the first American journalist expelled from Nazi Germany.

The co-joined village of Depew is part of the town of Lancaster. However, Depew had its own fire company and industries, including National Car Wheel Works, Gould Coupler Company, Union Car Company, Buffalo Cleaning and Dyeing Company and the Depew Brewing Company. Clearly, Depew was a blue-collar community. It was named for Chauncey M. Depew, president of the New York Central and Hudson River Railroad.

Williamsville

Located on Route 5, Williamsville is one of Buffalo's busiest suburbs. It was named for early settler Jonas Williams. Its growth began where the roads to Batavia and Buffalo crossed Ellicott Creek, namely because Glens Falls was a perfect location for mills to be built and the site of a convenient ford.

Of course, Jonas Williams built the first mill, Williamsville Water Mill. Glancing over the wall one can see what remains of the old raceway that powered the mills. Following tradition, Oziel Smith built a tavern and inn in 1832; it became a stagecoach stop, and the Eagle House is a popular restaurant today. Another early tavern and stagecoach stop that still remains is Glen Park Tavern, built in 1887. Eagle House and Glen Park Tavern are located on Main Street, Route 5.

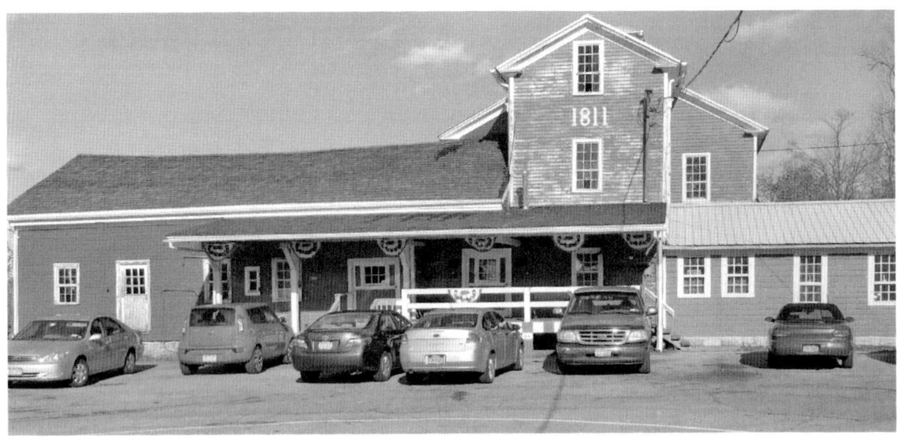

Williamsville Mill. *Courtesy of the author.*

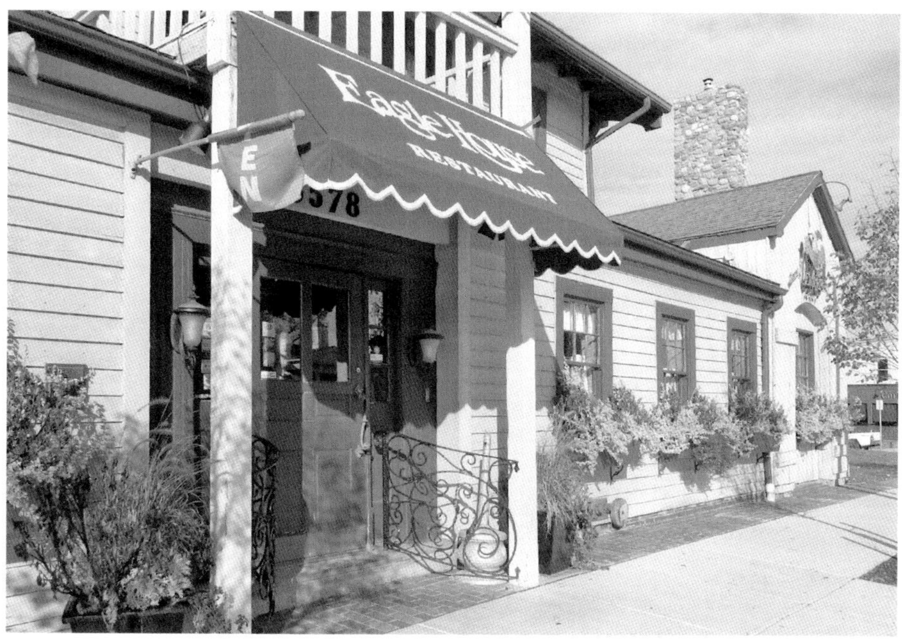

Eagle House. *Courtesy of the author.*

American troops camped in Williamsville during the War of 1812. This camp included a hospital and barracks. Soldiers who did not survive are buried in a small cemetery on Aero Drive.

Williamsville also valued education and built Williamsville Classical Institute in 1853. Studies took place over a three-year period, with three terms per year, placing the school way ahead of its time. There might have been one or more earlier schools, perhaps located in homes. That legacy of fine education continues.

Two of the village's most unique historic buildings are the Motherhouse and Oechsner Castle.

The Motherhouse is what locals call Saint Mary of the Angels Motherhouse complex. The convent was designed in 1928 for the Sisters of Saint Francis, housing nuns until it closed in 1998. It is remarkable because of its size in a residential community that still emulates its early origins. Dietel and Wade, who designed Buffalo's famed city hall, designed the convent. John Blocher, benefactor of Blocher Homes for the Elderly, donated the land on which the convent stood. Convent grounds are today's Amherst State Park. A portion of the site is senior housing and a chapel. The Sisters of Saint Francis of Assisi began their work in western New York in 1861.

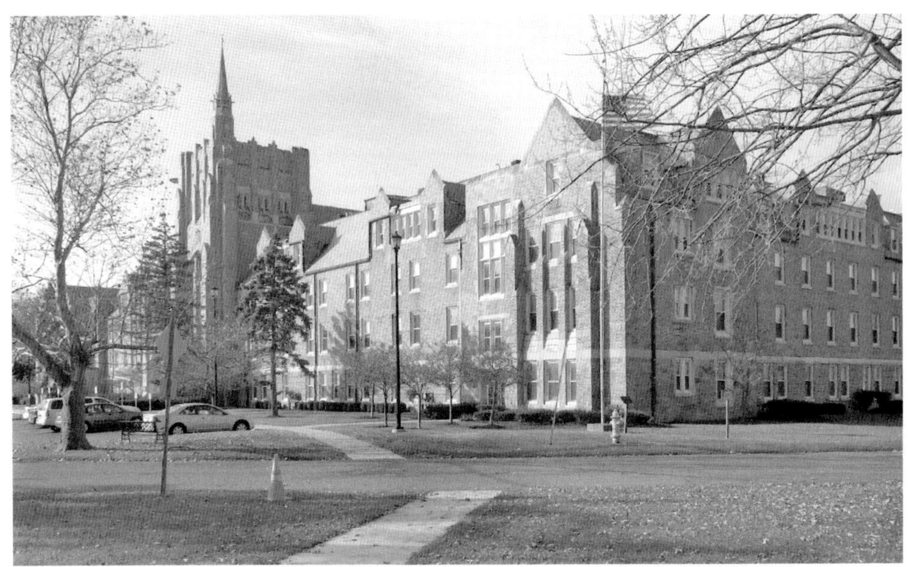

Saint Mary of the Angels Motherhouse, senior residence. *Courtesy of the author.*

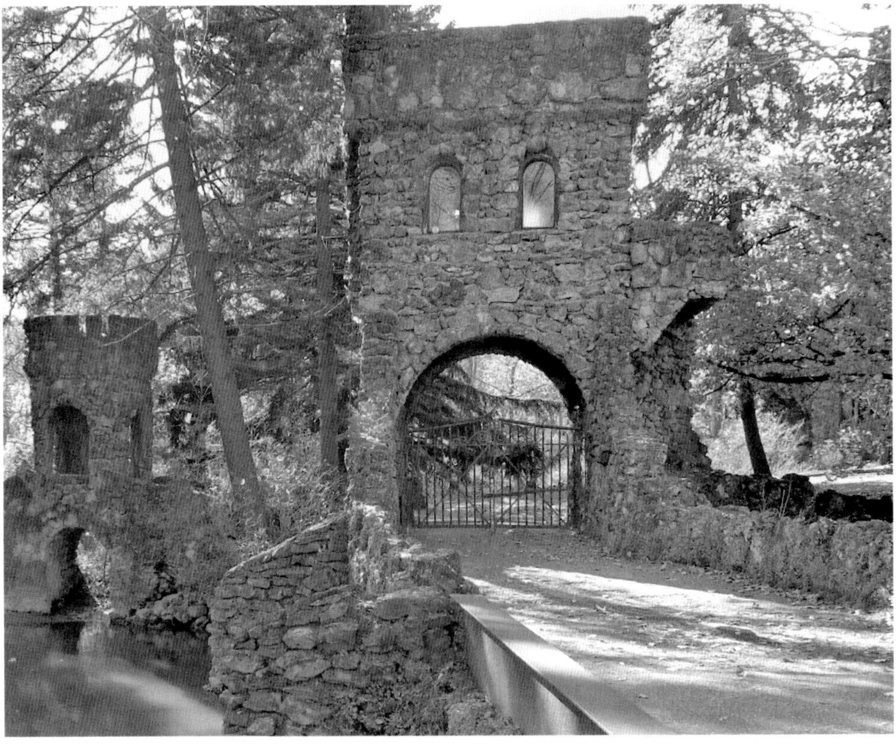

Oescher Castle gate, private residence. *Courtesy of the author.*

Oechsner Castle, on the other hand, is noteworthy because castles just aren't usually built in residential American neighborhoods. Built in 1917 by a German craftsman, Oechsner Castle is located on a small island complete with moat and bridge. Oechsner designed his castle after one in his homeland. Stone used for building it was imported from nearby Holland, New York. A fire in 1956 destroyed much of the castle's interior, but it was restored. Remarkably, this castle is not abandoned. This beautiful home is not accessible to the public, although one can catch a glimpse through the trees.

Cheektowaga: Jiikdowahgah (Land of Crabapples)

The earliest inhabitants were natives known as the Neuters (or Neutrals). The Senecas supplanted these early peoples and made the land their hunting and fishing grounds. The large Indian village of Gaskosada was located on the banks of Cayuga Creek, running through the town. Cheektowaga was obtained from the natives as part of the Treaty of Big Tree.

Both Williamsville and Cheektowaga were originally formed out of the town of Amherst. Cheektowaga's formation dates to 1829, though settlers began to arrive as early as 1808. The first was Apollo Hitchcock from Schenectady. Hitchcock's family ran successful farms, mills and a distillery for many decades.

The usual early industries also included a wool mill that burned, along with a sawmill in 1844. Cheektowaga experienced the German immigration that other towns had in 1830. The town grew slowly because larger communities around it drew the populations.

Interestingly, the main source of income for Cheektowaga residents during these early days was farming vegetables to be sold in the Buffalo market. Cheektowaga was a rural community. However, it was the railroad that finally helped the town prosper.

While an experiment to build residences between two railroads failed, the Delaware, Lackawanna and Western Railroad shops of 1890 finally did the trick. They drew employees and businesses. This became the village of Sloan, an offshoot of Cheektowaga.

Cheektowaga experienced its largest growth following World War II, when many communities built housing developments for returning soldiers. The now-demolished Westinghouse and Curtiss Wright plants were major sources of employment for many years. In fact, it was at Curtiss Wright that the D-40 aircraft flown by the famous Flying Tigers was manufactured.

Cheektowaga/West Seneca is also host to a long-standing popular business, Mayer Brothers cider mill. The company was founded in 1852, and local grocers still sell their products to this day. Visiting the mill and buying their cider is a western New York autumn tradition.

The population of Cheektowaga today includes a large Polish community.

Ebenezer Community of True Inspiration

Western New York history includes the years of the Burned-Over Districts south of the city of Buffalo. This was a movement of religious experimentation forming large portions of our landscape. However, the communities that grew out of this movement were not all that distant. Closer to Buffalo, Cheektowaga had a commune, too: the Ebenezer Community of True Inspiration.

Also known as Inspirationalists, the Ebenezer community consisted mostly of Germans who migrated here in 1843, along with Swiss and Austrians,

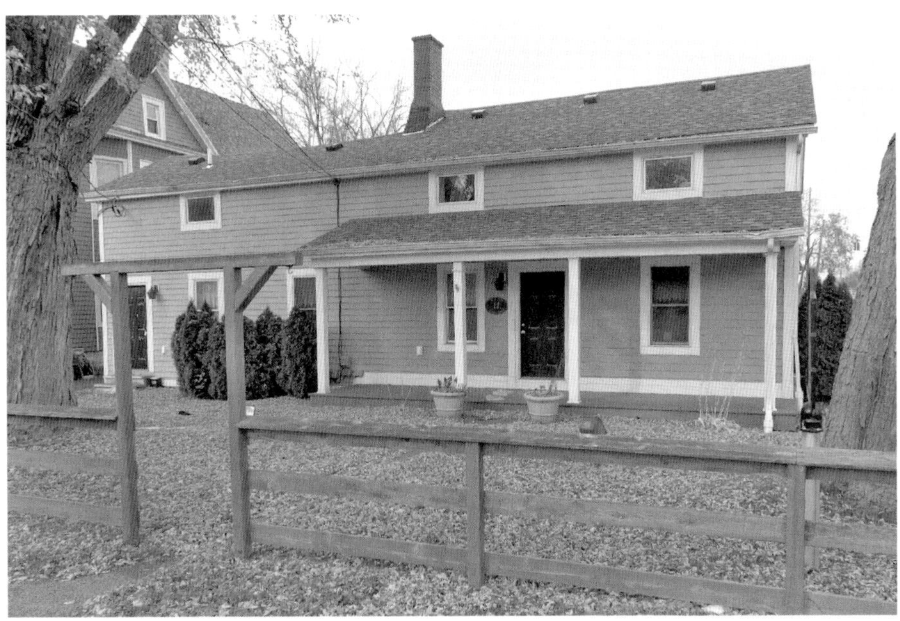

Leader of the Ebenezer Community Christian Metz's home. *Courtesy of the author.*

seeking a fresh approach to their religion. They split from the old Lutheran Church and had distinctive beliefs. They did not take oaths, serve in the military or send their children to state-run schools.

Persecuted in Germany for their ideologies, the Inspirationalists were arrested, their property damaged and their lives threatened. After moving to Hesse in Germany, where land, rent and the cost of living became unbearable, their leader, Christian Metz, traveled with a committee of three others to America to purchase land. America, the land of religious freedom, was their hope.

At first, the committee considered a tract of land near Chautauqua Lake but later settled on lands formerly owned by the Senecas in Cheektowaga, parts of which became current-day West Seneca and Elma. They bought the tract from the Ogden Land Company, made up mostly of speculators, who managed to "acquire" it from the Buffalo Creek Reservation. In truth, it was a fraudulent deal.

Very rural, Cheektowaga had plenty of room for the farm commune. Christian Metz named it Ebenezer—*eben* meaning "a stone," and *ezer* meaning "help" or "stone of help" in Hebrew. The hamlet of Ebenezer is today located at the crossroads of Union and Seneca Streets, though that is just a small portion of what it once held.

The Ebenezer settlement's early days were difficult. They cut trees, planted and built homes, a school and a meetinghouse (site of today's Fourteen Holy Helpers). However, Indians still living there were not happy with the intrusion. Getting them legally removed and paying the native community for peace was the Inspirationalists' solution. However, matters became complicated when the Ogden Company could not produce a legal deed for its purchase. Months of legal battles took place, but finally the Ebenezer community won its land. The Senecas were forced to leave, many going to the Cattaraugus Reservation.

Villages were already being settled within the tract, even before finalized deeds were received. A dam was built on Buffalo Creek to create a raceway for mills. In all, there were four separate villages with their own sustainable stores and other businesses. These were Middle Ebenezer (or Gardenville), Upper Ebenezer (which became Blossom), Lower Ebenezer and New Ebenezer (now Elma). Each village had a boundary cordoned off by footpaths to avoid interruption of day-to-day activities. Much planning was done to ensure an organized environment.

All members of Ebenezer were employed according to their abilities and interests. Profits, with the exception of clothing and household goods, were commune property. Some of the community's money went to buy passage to America for its members. All in all, it was the utopian ideal, with over eight hundred people migrating from Germany to live the way they believed. However, the perfect world they created for themselves was closing in.

By 1855, the original five thousand acres purchased had grown to eight thousand acres. This was largely farmland, and they liked it that way. However, the city of Buffalo was growing by leaps and bounds. It became impossible to maintain Ebenezer's autonomy and privacy. Christian Metz suggested that the Inspirationalists might be more inspired out west. By 1865, the remainder of the community had moved to Amana, Iowa.

Remnants of the commune's existence are seen in the hamlet of Ebenezer. Fourteen Holy Helpers Church was built over their meetinghouse. Additionally, there was the Heritage Inn, which has since burned. It was the bookbindery and eventual kitchen building, since Ebenezer homes did not have kitchens. Women and girls cooked in kitchen buildings throughout the community. A doctor's office was once the butcher shop, and other residences seen today were homes or sawmills. The Inspirationalists left a lasting footprint, though their presence has been mostly forgotten.

Buffalo: End of This Story

Although the westward trails of Routes 5 and 20 continue beyond Buffalo, it is here that our story ends. The city designed by Joseph Ellicott has a rich history that would fill many books and therefore cannot be written here. Buffalo has birthed artists; poets; inventors; U.S. presidents; and music, stage and screen and sports stars galore.

Water brought European explorers to Iroquois country—first by way of Lake Erie and the Niagara River and, later, the Erie Canal. As the western terminus of the Erie Canal, Buffalo has a history of both great wealth and a rougher nature. It was to Buffalo that many pioneers traveled, some staying while others refreshed their supplies before continuing on to Ohio. Many settled to work in Buffalo's various industries, from its grain elevators to its steel factories.

Beau Fleuve (Beautiful River), as named by the French, remains the second-largest city in New York State. Buffalo's size, architecture, ethnic blends and contributions to the growth and industry of a nation are ever present. The interminable spirit of the people living in Buffalo is as famed as its winter weather.

Three wars—the French and Indian War, the Revolution and the War of 1812—carved the region as surely as they did the state and the country.

Anchoring the state with Albany at the other end, famed and treed, the "City of Good Neighbors" continues the legacy begun by these early people of courage, preserving the past while looking to the horizon for the next great adventure.

It is said, "People may leave Buffalo, but Buffalo never leaves the people."

SELECTED BIBLIOGRAPHY

Websites

http://conservation.catholic.org/kateri.htm
http://localhistory.morrisville.edu/mhpc/history.html
https://ritdml.rit.edu
http://web.cortland.edu/woosterk/ononcent.html
http://xroads.virginia.edu
limahistorical.com
www.abneradamshouse.com
www.accessgenealogy.com
www.albanyny.gov/Government/CityHistory.aspx
www.alleylaw.net/nyonondaga.html
www.americanancestors.org/early-palatine-families-of-new-york
www.americanhoteloflima.com
www.amsterdamny.gov/visitors/about-amsterdam.php
www.archive.org
www.avonhistorical.org
www.avon-ny.org
www.beekman1802.com/the-loomis-gang
www.bigspringsmuseum.org
www.biographi.ca
www.bloomfieldny.org
www.britannica.com
www.carf.info
www.catholic.org/saints
www.cephasministry.com/evangelists_william_branham_11.html
www.cityofschenectady.com/history.html

www.clintonhistory.org
www.co.montgomery.ny.us
www.co.seneca.ny.us
www.co.wayne.ny.us
www.dmna.ny.gov/forts
www.earlyamerica.com
www.eco.canadiana.ca
www.edyoungs.com
www.elim.edu/history
www.en.wikipedia.org
www.eriecanal.org
www.erie.gov
www.ewtn.com
www.familysearch.org/learn/wiki/en/Great_Genesee_Road
www.findagrave.com/cgi-bin/fg.cgi?page=gr&GRid=25772458
www.fingerlakeshousehistories.com
www.fingerlakesphysicians.com/home/history.htm
www.fold3.com
www.fortherkimerchurch.org
www.fortklock.com
www.fort-plank.com
www.fulton.nygenweb.net
www.funding universe.com/company-histories
www.ganondagan.org
www.genevahistoricalsociety.com
www.ghosttowns.com
www.gotquestions.org/latter-rain-movement.html
www.hallofgovernors.ny.gov
www.heapsofhistory.blogspot.com
www.herkimer.nygenweb.net
www.historiccherryvalley.com
www.history.com/this-day-in-history
www.history.rays-place.com
www.historystarproductions.com
www.indiancastle.com
www.indiantime.net
www.institutionalgreen.org
www.jellogallery.org
www.kateritekakwitha.org
www.lifeinthefingerlakes.com
www.lincklaenhouse.com/history.html
www.linwoodgardens.org
www.littlefallsny.com
www.livingplaces.com
www.lorenzony.org/history

www.madisoncounty.ny.gov
www.math.buffalo.edu/~sww/0history/hwny-tubman.html
www.montgomery.nygenweb.net
www.mpaulkeeslerbooks.com
www.muiniskw.org
www.netplaces.com/american-revolution
www.newadvent.org/cathen/04732a.htm
www.newrivernotes.com
www.newyorktraveler.net
www.nps.gov/history
www.nps.gov/nr
www.nycanals.com
www.nyfalls.com
www.nyhistoric.com
www.nyhistory.net
www.nysasylum.com
www.nysm.nysed.gov
www.nysm.nysed.gov/albany/bios/j/swj.html
www.oldpalatinechurch.org
www.oneidacity.com/Our%20Community/our%20community.html
www.oneidacommunity.org
www.onlinebiographies.info
www.oswego.edu/library2/archives
www.pacny.net/freedom_trail
www.puffin.creighton.edu/jesuit/relations
www.revolutionaryday.com
www.rollinghillsasylum.vpweb.com
www.rootsweb.ancestry.com/~nytryon/tryonmil.html
www.sacred-texts.com
www.schenectadyhistory.org
www.scout.me/history-and-heritage--near--caledonia-ny
www.senecafalls.com
www.sfhistoricalsociety.org
www.skaneatelesluxuryvacationrentals.com/blog/the-rich-history-of-skaneateles-lake
www.sonnenberg.org
www.staffordhistoricalsociety.org www.stisaac.org
www.syracusethenandnow.org
www.thehollowayhouse.com
www.thelcn.com
www.threeriversh ms.com
www.tocny.org/home/townhistory.aspx
www.townofbatavia.com
www.townofbethany.com
www.townofcanandaigua.org
www.townofdarienny.com

www.townofeastbloomfield.com
www.townofelbridge.com
www.townofpembroke.org
www.uppercanadahistory.ca/puc/puc4.html
www.u-s-history.com
www.village.herkimer.ny.us
www.villageofelbridge.com
www.villageofvernonny.org/history.html
www.watervilleny.com
www.westseneca.com
www.woodwardmemoriallibrary.org
www.wyandot.org
www.yeoldelandmark.com
www2.erie.gov/parks

Books

Ainsworth, Catherine. *Legends of New York State*. Buffalo, NY: Clyde Press, 1978.

Althouse, Peter. "Spirit of the Last Days: Pentecostal Eschatology in Conversation with Jurgen Moltmann." *Journal of Pentecostal Theology Supplement.* First edition. New York: Bloomsbury Academic, 2003.

Berkin, Carol. *Revolutionary Mothers: Women in the Struggle for American Independence*. New York: Vintage Books, 2003.

Czarnota, Lorna. *Legends, Lore and Secrets of Western New York*. Charleston, SC: The History Press, 2009.

———. *Wicked Niagara: The Sinister Side of the Niagara Frontier*. Charleston, SC: The History Press, 2011.

Eckert W., Allan. *The Wilderness War*. New York: Bantam Books, 1978.

Koelher, Carl Andrew. *Talking Trees & Spirit Trails: New York State Native American Trail Trees*. Charleston, SC: CreateSpace, an Amazon Co., 2013.

Laramie, Michael. *The European Invasion of North America: Colonial Conflict Along the Hudson-Champlain Corridor, 1690–1760.* Westport, CT: Praeger, 2012.

Martin, Rafe. *Rough-Face Girl*. New York: Putnam Berkley Group, 1992.

O'Keefe, Rose. *Historic Genesee Country: A Guide to Its Lands and Legacies*. Charleston, SC: The History Press, 2010.

Thurheimer C., David. *Landmarks of the American Revolution in New York State*. Albany: New York State American Revolution Bicentennial Commission, 1974.

INDEX

O

P

Q

R

S

T

U

V

W

ABOUT THE AUTHOR

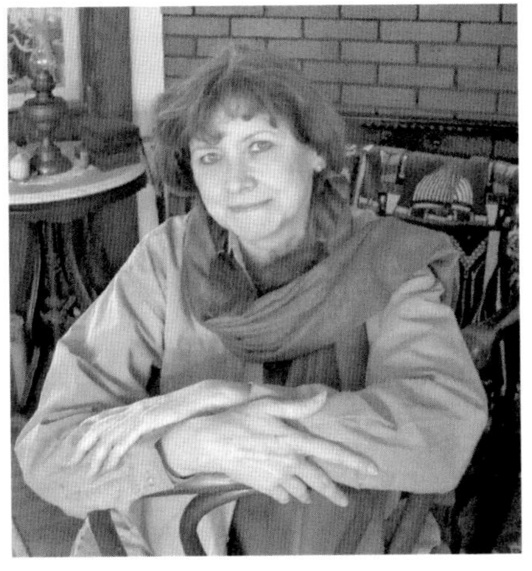

"On the road again" best describes author and storyteller Lorna MacDonald Czarnota's love of history. Ever ready with a story, Lorna prefers whenever she can to visit historical and mythological sites. Her work has taken her across New York State and elsewhere in the United States, Canada, Scotland and Ireland. Her award-winning storytelling has been featured in schools and libraries and at festivals and conferences.

Lorna is the author of *Breadline Blue*; *Legends, Lore and Secrets of Western New York*; *Wicked Niagara: The Sinister Side of the Niagara Frontier*; and *Medieval Tales that Kids Can Read and Tell.* Her short stories and articles appear in several anthologies and magazines. Her book and guidebooks on using story to mentor at-risk youth are forthcoming with Parkhurst Brothers in 2014.

Additional photographs and information may be found on Lorna's website: www.lornamacdonaldczarnota.com.